Thomas Fuller

The marvellous wisdom and quaint conceits of Thomas Fuller

Thomas Fuller

The marvellous wisdom and quaint conceits of Thomas Fuller

ISBN/EAN: 9783337281724

Printed in Europe, USA, Canada, Australia, Japan

Cover: Foto ©Andreas Hilbeck / pixelio.de

More available books at **www.hansebooks.com**

THE MARVELLOUS WISDOM AND QUAINT CONCEITS OF THOMAS FULLER, D.D., BEING ".THE HOLY STATE." SOMEWHAT ABRIDGED AND SET IN ORDER BY ADELAIDE L. J. GOSSET.

WHEREUNTO IS ADDED "THE FIRST BIOGRAPHY" OF "THE DOCTOR OF FAMOUS MEMORY."

LONDON. PICKERING AND CHATTO, 66, HAY-MARKET. ANNO. DOM. MDCCCXCIII.

CHISWICK PRESS:—C. WHITTINGHAM AND CO., TOOKS COURT,
CHANCERY LANE.

CONTENTS.

THE HOLY STATE.

FOREWORD.

THE
L I F E
OF

That Reverend Divine

AND

Learned Hiſtorian,

Dr. THOMAS FULLER.

Si Poſt Fata venit Gloria ſic propero,
Mart.

LONDON.
Printed for J. W. H. B. and H. M.
1661.

TO THE READER.

THIS reverend person deceased, who whiie he shined here gave a full meridian light to all kind of history, sets with this shadow in his own, the dark side of that lanthorn to himself, whose lucidations had discovered all before it, and rescued so many brave memories from the violence of time. Pity it is that such excellent persons (for it is their common fate) should be so neglectful of themselves, while they are so serviceable to the world, which reaps all with a careless or ungrateful return to the authors of their store and increase. And as the intrinsic worth of diamonds exerts not its lustre without a foil, so it fareth with the most costly and rich shrines of those resplendent and shining virtues erected in the memory and fame of worthy men, which are always showed by lamp; or some other efficacious and borrowed light, that only directs to the solemnity and invites veneration, but cannot contribute nor add any real estimate and honour to the saint himself. The account of this reverend doctor deceased states itself on this apology;

it pretends not to be any of his least and inconsider-
able relic, and it doth alike justify itself from being
his legend, merely the worth of so deserving a person,
(which no pen hath yet undertook or attempted) for
civilities sake, hath obliged this essay, which to your
easiest censure is here submitted.

VALE.

THE LIFE OF

THE REVEREND AND EXCELLENT DOCTOR

THOMAS FULLER.

THE ample subject of this incompetent relation is doctor Thomas Fuller, to whose dust we do avowedly consecrate this eulogy the doctor of famous memory.

He was born at Alwinde an obscure town in Northamptonshire, some five miles from Oundle in the year of our Lord 16 . . [1608] a place now equal to, and vying honour with any seed-plot (in that country) of virtue, learning and religion, and of which hereafter to its glory it shall be said, *that this man was born there*. He was the son of Mr. Tho. Fuller, the minister of the same town, a man of a blameless and as private life, who spent himself in the discharge of his pastoral office to which God had called him, without embarking himself in the busy controversies of his time, that laboured under the fatigues of most importunate puritanism and pleading popery. Part of this privacy bestowed itself fruitfully upon the youth of the venerable doctor, (who had lost some time under the ill menage of a raw and unskilful schoolmaster) so that in a little space such a proficiency was visibly seen in him, that it was a question whether he owed more to his father for his birth or education; both which had so happily and so easily concurred that he was admirably learned before it could be supposed he had been taught; and this will seem no paradox to those who knew his felicity of memory which he owed not to the lubricity of art, but the certainty of nature.

Having under this tuition past the just time of adolescency in those puerile studies, at twelve years of age, this hopeful slip was translated to Cambridge, where he first settled in Queen's College of which a near kinsman of his Dr. . . [Davenent] was then president. This was a sphere wherein his relucent virtues and conspicuous abilities had room to exert themselves, so that he filled the eyes of the university with a just expectation of his future lustre.

Here he successively passed the degrees of bachelor and master of arts, with such general commendation, and at such unusual age that such a commencement was not within memory. During his residence in this college a fellowship was vacant, for which the doctor became candidate, prompted thereunto by a double plea of merit and interest, beside the desire of the whole house; but a statute of the college prevailing against them all, which admitted not two fellows of the said county of Northampton, the doctor quitted his pretensions and designation to that preferment. And though he was well assured of a dispensation from the strict limitation of that statute to be obtained for him, yet he totally declined it, as not willing to owe his rise and advancement to the courtesy of so ill a precedent, that might usher in more immodest intrusions upon the privileges and laws of the college.

But this gave him a fair occasion to transfer himself to Sidney College, whither by some of his choice and learned friends, he had often been invited. He had not been long here, but he was chosen minister of St. Bennet's parish in the town of Cambridge, in whose church he offered the primitie of his ministerial fruits, which like *apples of gold in pictures of silver* (sublime divinity in the most ravishing elegancies) attracted the audience of the university, by whose dilated commendations, he was generally known at that age at which most men do but peep into the world. These his great sufficiences (being now but about the age of twenty-three years) tendered him a prebendary of Salisbury, and at the same time a fellowship in Sidney college. They were both eximious preferments as the times then were, the estimation of either being

b

equally great *mutatis mutandis* but the doctor's inclination biassed him to the more active and profitable incumbency; into which his inbred piety and devotion had from the first of his resolutions inducted him. Whereupon he retired from that university and betook himself to the priestly function, being thereunto ordained by the right reverend father in God the bishop of Salisbury.

This being the king's donation, was some further reason for abandoning his most pleasant studies and conversation in Cambridge, for that also by the statutes of both universities it is provided that no person who shall have ten pounds per annum in the king's books shall be capable of a fellowship in either of them. So Providence was pleased to dispose of him in each of these academical honorary intendments, that his fluent should not run silently in those streams and contribute only to their emanations, but with fame discharge itself into the ocean, and reciprocate honour and desert with the world. Having thus launched, and being so furnished, he set forth in the course of the ministry, exchanging those delightful privacies of his college studies (which laid the happy foundations and beginnings of those excellent books which successively teemed those productions and propagations of divine learning and knowledge, of which more hereafter,) for the troublesome cure of a parish and importunate pulpit. That prebend of Salisbury was a commodious step to another more profitable place, which for its vicinity to that cathedral, and being in the same diocese, did easily commend itself without the aid and instance of the patron, or other inducements to the doctor's acceptance; but yet he did not over-readily entertain the kindness of the proffer till after a serious scrutiny of himself and his abilities to discharge the requisite duties the place called for; and after a very full and satisfactory enquiry of his parishioners. It was the rectory of Broad Windsor in Dorsetshire, a place far distanced from his native country and remoter from his university. *A prophet hath no honour in his own;* and therefore it was doubled to him in another. The accommodation both in reference to his maintenance and respect from this people was very noble, and which afforded great expedience to the doctor's other labours, which were bountifully cherished under the tuition of his ministry. After some while employed here in the pastoral office, the doctor was desired by some friends to dignify his desert with the degree which his time and standing by the rules of the university afforded him : whereunto the doctor out of a reverence to his honourable calling was well inclined, and accordingly prepared for his departure to Cambridge to take the degree of bachelor of divinity. Having taken care therefore to supply his place for the time of his absence, at his setting forth he was acquainted that four of his chief parishioners with his good leave were ready to wait on him to Cambridge, to testify their exceeding engagements, it being the sense and request of his whole parish. This kindness was so present and so resolutely pressed, that the doctor with many thanks for that and other demonstrations of their love towards him, gladly accepted of their company, and with his customary innate pleasantness entertained their time to the journey's end.

At his coming to Cambridge he was most welcomely treated and saluted by his friends and acquaintance, and visited almost by all considerable persons of the university and town ; especially of his parishioners of St. Bennet: fame and love vying which should render him most addresses, to the great delight and satisfaction of his fellow-travellers and neighbours in having a minister who was so highly and yet no less deservedly honoured, but to the trouble of the modest doctor, who was then forced to busy his invention with compliments, to which he was most naturally averse. At this commencement there proceeded with him in the same degree of bachelor of divinity three

other reverend persons, all with general applause and
commendation ; and therefore to do them no wrong
must forbear to give the deceased doctor his particular
due. Only thus much by the way may be added, that
this commencement cost the doctor for his particular
the sum of sevenscore pounds, and evidence of his
liberality and largeness of mind proportionable to his
other capacities, and yet then which nothing was less
studied. At his departure he was dismissed with as
honourable valedictions, and so he returned in the
same company (who had out of their own purse con-
tributed another addition of honour to that solemnity)
to his said rectory at Broad Winsor resolving there to
spend himself and the time of his pilgrimage amongst
his dear and loving charge. In the amenity and re-
tirements of this rural life some perfection was given
to those pieces which soon after blest this age, (an
account of all which is reserved to the conclusion of
these collections), from this pleasant prospect he drew
that excellent piece of the *Holy Land Pisgah Sight*,
and other tracts relating thereunto, so that what was
said bitterly of some tyrants, that they made whole
countries vast solitudes and deserts, may be inverted
to the eulogy of this doctor, that he in these recesses
made deserts the solitudes of Israel, the frequented
path and track of all ingenuous and studious persons.

But contemplation and the immurement of his vast
spirit within the precincts of his parish (although both
delightful and profitable those foreign travels of his
brain above mentioned affording the one, and his
pious labours at home yielding the other) grew tedious
and wearisome to his active and free genius, which
was framed by nature for converse and general intelligence, not to be smothered in such an obscurity.
To this inclination also the unquietness and trepida-
tions of those times (then scared with the news of a
war about religion and reformation which the Scots
pretended) did oversway him. He was very sensible
whither those first commotions did tend, and that
some heavy disaster did in those angry clouds which
impended over the nation, more particularly threaten
the clergy. He was then also married unto a vertuous
young gentlewoman, and by her had born there, his
eldest son, now a hopeful plant in the same college and
university where his father had his education. These
motives concurring with that general fame and esteem
of him, drew him to the consultation of a city life,
where both security, honour, and the advantages of
learning, did demonstratively promise the completion
of his desires, and intended tranquillity, destined
already to some public works which were then in
designment. Removing therefore to London, having

obtained his fair dismission from that charge in the
country, he continued his pious endeavours of preaching in most of the voiced pulpits of London (being
cried up for one of the most excellent preachers of his
age) but most usually in the inns of court.

He was from thence by the master and brotherhood
of the Savoy (as well as earnestly desired and intreated
by that small parish) complemented to accept of the
lecturer's place, which having undertaken after some
instance he did most piously and effectually discharge,
witness the great confluence of affected hearers from
distant congregations, insomuch that his own cure
were (in a sense) excommunicated from the church,
unless their timous diligence kept pace with their
devotion; the doctor affording them no more time for
their extraordinaries on the Lord's day, then what he
allowed his habituated abstinence on all the rest. He
had in his narrow chapel two audiences, one without
the pale, the other within the windows of that little
church, and the sextonry so crowded, as if bees had
swarmed to his mellifluous discourse. He continued
here to the great satisfaction of his people, and the
neighbouring nobility and gentry, till our unhappy
unnatural wars had made a dismal progress through
the whole nation : labouring all that while in private
and in public, to beget a right understanding among

all men of the king's most righteous cause, which
through seduction and popular fury was generally
maligned. His exhortations to peace and obedience
were his constant subjects in the church, (all his
sermons were such liturgies) while his secular days
were spent in vigorously promoting the king's affairs
either by a sudden reconciliation, or potent assistance.
To this end on the anniversary day of his late majesty's
inauguration, which was the . . [27] day of March, 1642,
he preached at St. Peter's, Westminster, on this text,
2. Sam. xix. 30, *Yea let him take all, so that my lord
the king return in peace.* A theme so distasteful to
the ringleaders of the rebellion (who had on purpose
so scandalously driven him from his court and parliament that he might never with any pleasure think of
returning to them till he had vindicated his honour
upon the abettors of those tumults) and so well and
loyally enforced by him, that drew not only a suspicion
from the moderate mislead party of parliament, but
an absolute odium on him from the grandees and
principals in the rebellion. There were few or none
of the orthodox clergy then remaining within their
lines of communication, (new invented limits for the
city's old liberties,) some being dead in restraint, or
through more harsh, and cruel dealing, the rest outed
and silenced ; so that their inspection and espial was

confined almost to the doctor's pulpit as to public
assemblies; where nevertheless he desisted not nor
altered from his main course, the doctrine of allegiance,
till such time as the covenant was obtruded upon his
conscience, and must through his persuasions be likewise pressed upon his people.   Several false rumours
and cavils there are about his carriage and opinion
touching that sacrilegious thing by persons who were
distanced as far from the knowledge of those passages
as fortunately from being concerned and engaged
within the reach of that snare.   'Twas not only easy
but most prudential, for other ecclesiastical persons
to quit their livings, who were out of the grips
and clutches of those ravenous reformists in order to
keep their consciences inviolable; but it was difficulty
enough of itself for the doctor to escape and get out
of that place, where the next preferment would have
been a dungeon. Some velilations transient discourses
he made about that frequent and thumbed subject
of the reformation, the rather to suspend the busy
censures of the parliament and their party, wherein
though he seemed to comply but as far as the rule and
example would allow and indulge the misapprehension
of those men, yet these his charitable disguises could
not obscure him from the severe animadversions of
several ministers eminent in those reforming times,

particularly Mr. Saltmarsh. The contest betwixt them is so known in print, that it will be needless to trouble the reader with it here : only thus much by digression in honour of this venerable doctor : Mr. Saltmarsh being long since dead, he hath in his book of *The Worthies General of England* (of which here-after) given him a most honourable mention, and assigned him the place of his birth, education, and burial, registering him for an ornament of them all ; so resplendent and durable was the doctor's charity. I may not omit one thing, that the doctor in record-ing and relating of the death of the said Mr. Saltmarsh, doth passionately reflect on the shortness of his life and the acuteness of that fever which so violently ended him, reducing and applying it to the un-certainty of his own state, and we now unhappily see those curious presages of his pen verified and accom-plished in his most immature and sudden decease.

To return to our subject, in the beginning of the year 1643 the said Covenant was generally pressed, and a very great persecution soon after followed it. The doctor was settled in the love and affections of his own parish, besides other obligations to his nume-rous followers ; so that the Covenant then tendered might seem like the bright side of that cloud (promis-ing serenity and prosperity to him, as was insinuated to the doctor by many great parliamentarians) which showered down after a little remoteness, such a black horrible tempest upon the clergy, nay the church and three kingdoms. But the good doctor could not bow down his knee to that *Baal-Berith*, nor for any worldly considerations (enough whereof invited him even to fall down and worship, men of his great parts being infinitely acceptable to them) lend so much as an ear to their serpentine charms of religion and reformation.

Since therefore he could not continue with his cure without his conscience, and every day threatened the imposition of that illegal Oath, he resolved to betake himself to God's providence, and to put himself directly under it, waiving all indirect means and advantages whatsoever towards his security. In order thereunto, in April 1643 he deserted the City of London, and privately conveyed himself to Oxford, to the no less sudden amazement of the faction here, who yet upon recollection quickly found their mistake, then to the unexpected content and joy of the loyal party there, who had every day Job's messengers of the plundering, ruins and imprisonments of orthodox divines. Oxford was then the common refuge and shelter of such perse-cuted persons, so that it never was, nor is like to be, a more learned university, nor did ever letters and arms so well consist together it being an accomplished academy of both.

Among the multitude of those new comers like the clean beasts to the ark when the waters increased, the king (the most excellent intelligent prince of the abilities of his clergy) vouchsafed the doctor the honour of preaching before him in St. Mary's, where with the like moderation he laid open the blessings of an accommodation, as being too sensible and that so recently of the virulency and impotent rage, though potent arms, of the disloyal Londoners : which as the doctor then christianly thought could not better be allayed than by a fair condiscension in matters of church reformation. It seems some particulars in that sermon gave offence to some at court, as if the good doctor were a lukewarm royalist, and did not throughly own his majesty's cause, which ill grounded conceit (though he were well satisfied in that his plea for composure) did not a little trouble him: to explain and free himself, an opportunity was wanting both of press and pulpit, and the hurry of the war gave not his prejudiced hearers leasure for his particular vindication. He resolved therefore strenuously to evince his faithful loyalty to the king by another kind of argument, by appearing in the king's armies, to be a preacher militant to his soldiers. This resolution Providence was pleased to favour by an honourable friend's recommendation of the doctor to my lord Hopton, who was then to choose a chaplain. This noble lord though as courageous and expert a captain, and successful withal as the king had any, was never averse to an amicable closure of the war upon fair and honourable terms, and did therefore well approve of the doctor and his desire and pursuit after peace. The good doctor was likewise infinitely contented in his attendance on such an excellent personage, whose conspicuous and noted loyality could not but derive the same reputation to his retainers, especially one so near his conscience as his chaplain, and so wipe off that stain which the mistakes of those men had cast on him. In this entendment God was pleased to succeed the doctor and give him victory (proper to the camp he followed), against this first attempt on his honour.

During the campania, and while the army continued in the field, he performed the duty of his holy function, with as much solemn piety and devotion as he used before in places consecrated to God's worship ; and according to the form used and appointed by the Church of England. In all emergencies and present Enterprizes using no other prayers, than what the care of the fathers of the Church had in those miserable exigences newly directed. To this he added constant preaching on the Lord's day, animating in his sermons the soldiers to fight courageously, and to demean themselves worthy of that glorious cause with which God had honoured them.

With the progress of the war he marched from place to place and wherever there happened for the better accommodation of the army any reasonable stay he allotted it with great satisfaction to his beloved studies. Those cessations and intermissions begot in him the most intentness and solicitous industry of mind, which as he never used to much recreation or diversion in times of peace, which might loose and relax a well disciplined spirit, so neither did the horror and rigidness of the war stiffen him in such a stupidity (which generally possessed all learned men,) or else distract him, but that in such lucid intervals he would seriously and fixedly, come to himself and his designed business. Indeed his business and study then, was a kind of errantry having proposed to himself a more exact collection of the *Worthies General of England* and in which others had waded before, but he resolved to go through. In what place soever therefore he came of remark especially, he spent frequently most of his time in views and researches of their anti-

quities and church monuments, insinuating himself into
the acquaintance (which frequently ended in a lasting
friendship) of the learnedst and gravest persons resid-
ing within the place, thereby to inform himself fully
of those things he thought worthy the commendation
of his labours.   It is an incredible thing to think what
a numerous correspondence the doctor maintained
and enjoyed by this means.

Nor did the good doctor ever refuse to light his
candle in investigating truth from the meanest person's discovery.   He would endure contentedly, an
hour or more impertinence from any aged church
officer, or other superannuated people for the gleaning
of two lines to his purpose.   And though his spirit
was quick and nimble, and all the faculties of his
mind ready, and answerable, to that activity of dispatch, yet in these inquests he would stay and attend
those circular rambles till they come to a point, so
resolute was he bent to the sifting out of abtruse
antiquity.   Nor did he ever dismiss any such feeble
adjutators or helpers (as he pleased to style them)
without giving them money and cheerful thanks
besides.   After the fight at Cheriton Down my lord
Hopton drew down with his army and artillery to
Basing and so marched that way to Oxford, intend-
ing to take up winter quarters as soon as he had con-

sulted with the king, and left the doctor in that as
courageously manned, as well fortified house where
he had scarce begun to reduce his marching observations into form and method, but Sir William Waller
having taken in Winchester, came to besiege the
doctor's sanctuary.   This no way amated or terrified
him, but only the noise of the cannon playing from
the enimies leaguer interrupted the prosecution of
digesting his notes, which trouble he recompenced to
them by an importunate spiriting of the defendants in
their sallies ; which they followed so close and so
bravely, suffering the besiegers scarce to eat and sleep,
that Sir William was compelled to raise the siege, and
march away leaving above a thousand men slain
behind him ; and the doctor the pleasure of seeing that
strong effort of rebellion in some way by his means
repulsed and defeated, and in being free to proceed
in his wonted intendments.   What time the doctor
continued here is very uncertain, sure we may be, he
was not unemployed, or an unacceptable guest to that
loyal garrison, and that as noble and honourable
Marquis the proprietary of the place ; the demolish-
ing of which princely edifice then standing in spite of
their potent arms, yet afterwards through the fortune
of war being fallen into their hands and razed by their
more impotent revenge, he doth heartily lament in his

Worthies General preferring it while it flourished for the chiefest fabric in Hampshire. This his kindness to the place of his refuge though no doubt true and deserved enough, yet no questionless was endeared in him by some more peculiar obliging regards and respects he found during his abode there, though indeed his worth could want and miss them nowhere. The next removal of the doctor was to his charge in the army, and his particular duty of chaplain to his said lord. The war was then at its zenith, hotter and more dilated, raging everywhere, both in this and the two neighbouring kingdoms, so that there was no shelter or retirement which it had not invaded and intruded into by unruly garrisons, while the country became a devested solitude, so that the doctor's design could proceed nowhere. But that fatal war hasteing to a sad and miserable end, success not answering the merit of the cause, the king's field-forces being every where engaged, and part of the loyal army driven into Cornwall under the command of that skilful captain, the good doctor took refuge betimes in Exeter, having taken his congé and dismission of his beloved lord.

Here again he resumed his task of the aforesaid *Worthies*, not minding the cloud impending on that place, nor no way intermitting the duty of his calling;

preaching constantly to those truly loyal citizens. It is a supernumary labour to acquaint the reader with how great satisfaction and content, that always and everywhere being annexed to his meanest endeavours.

During his stay at Exeter, the Queen having been delivered of her last burden (saving her sorrows and distresses) by the birth of the princess Henrietta, the learned doctor was preferred to be the infant lady's chaplain. Her royal father's intendment being, as he had educated the rest of his princely issue, to have her brought up in the protestant religion. To that end, the good doctor in regard of his soundness and sincerity in that profession and eminent famous assertion of it, was designed to attend on her, to instil unto her tender mind (if God had pleased to continue her with safety within the limits of this kingdom) the principles and belief of the English (catholic) Church. This for the present was altogether honorary and pointed only at his merit, which indeed was as much as the iniquity of those times would afford to any the most deserving personages. But yet the king to signify his approbation of the doctor's excellent worth by a farther testimony of it, soon afterwards gave him a patent for his presentation to the town of Dorchester in Dorsetshire, a living valued to be worth £400 per annum, This royal and bounteous favour the doctor modestly declined, continuing his attendance on the princess till the rendition of the city of Exeter to the parliament. Notwithstanding the doctor accepted not of that other preferment of Dorchester, for that London was in his eye, as the most necessary and expedient place for finishing his aforesaid book, to which place the expiration of the war promised some kind of access, which since it could not otherwise be, the doctor did gladly submit to. For general Fairfax, having by treaty reduced and disbanded my lord Hopton's army in Cornwall came directly back to besiege Exeter, which garrison upon consideration that no relief could be expected, and that resistance would but defer the resettling of the king and kingdom (pressed also by the enemy as a cogent argument for their rendition) having very honourable and comprehensive articles, both for their conscience and estates, delivered up the city to the parliament forces. In these articles the doctor was included and by the benifit of them, was without molestation or hinderance permitted to come to the city of London, where he presently recommenced his labourious enterprize, and by the additional help of books, the confluence and resort of learned men his acquaintance, to their fleecing tyrannical courts and committees newly

erected made such a progress that from thence he
could take a fair prospect of his whole work. Upon
his first arrival he came *to his own* (the parish of
Savoy) *but they received him not*, the face of things
was so altered ; many of his parishioners dead, others
removed, all of them generally so overawed by an
imperious rabbi of both factions, presbytery and
independency. One Mr. Bond formerly a preacher
at Exeter, then made by the pretended powers master
of the Savoy (the doctor and he having counter-
marched and changed ground, wherein different seed
was sown of loyal obedience and treasonable sedition)
that the doctor might have said of his parish what a
learned historian said in another greater case *parochia
in parochia quærenda erat*. But a living was not the
design of the good doctor, who knew how incom-
patible the times and his doctrine must needs be.
However as oft as he had private opportunities he
ceased not to assert the purity of the Church of England, bewailing the sad condition into which the
grievous abominable sins of the nation had so far
plunged it, as to make it more miserable by bearing
so many reproaches and calumnies, grounded only
upon its calamity. But some glimmering hopes of a
settlement and understanding betwixt the king and
the pretended houses appearing, the pious doctor

betook himself to earnest prayers and petitions to God, that he would please to succeed that blessed work, doing that privately as a christian, which he might not publicly do as a subject, most fervently imploring in those families where his person and devotion were alike acceptable, the blessing of restoration on this afflicted Church, and its defenceless defender, the king.

That desired affair went on slowly and uncertainly, but so did not the doctor's book. For having recommended the first to the Almighty wisdom, he stood not still expecting the issue, but addressed himself to his study, affording no time but the leisure of his meals which was short, to the hearing of news, with which the minds and mouths of men were then full employed by the changeableness of the army who played fast and loose with the king and parliament, till in conclusion they destroyed both. Then indeed such an amazement struck the loyal pious doctor when he first heard of that execrable design intended against the king's person, and saw the villany proceed so uncontrollably, that he not only surceased but resolved to abandon that luckless work (as he was then pleased to call it) for what shall I write, said he, of *The Worthies of England*, when this horrid act will bring such an infamy upon the whole nation as will ever cloud and darken all its former, and suppress its future rising glories? But when through the feared impiety of those men, that parricide was perpetrated, the good doctor deserted not his study alone, but forsook himself too, not caring for, or regarding, his concerns (though the doctor was none of the most providential husband by having store beforehand) until such time as his prayers, tears, and fasting, having better acquainted him with that sad dispensation, he began to revive from that dead pensiveness to which he had so long addicted himself. He therefore now again renewed his former study, setting about it with unwearied diligence. About this time also it happened that the rectory of Waltham Abbey being vacant, and in the disposal of the right honourable Earl of Carlisle, since deceased, he voluntarily and desirously conferred it on the doctor, and together made him his chaplain, both which he very piously and profitably performed, being highly beloved by that noble lord, and other gentlemen and inhabitants of the parish. About this time also many of the orthodox clergy began to appear again in the pulpits of London through the zeal of some right worthy citizens, who hungered after the true and sincere word, from which they had so long been restrained; among the chief of whom was our good doctor, being settled lecturer

for a time at St. Clement's Lane near Lumbard,
Street where he preached every Wednesday in the
afternoon, to a very numerous and christian audience,
and shortly after from thence he was removed to
St. Bride's in Fleet Street in the same quality of
lecturer, the day being changed to Thursday, where
he preached with the same efficacy and success.

The doctor having continued some 12 years a
widower, the war finding him so, had the better
relished the loss of his first wife, by how much the
freer it rendered him of care and trouble for her in
those troublesome times, so as by degrees it had
almost settled in him a persuasion of keeping himself
in that state. But now an honourable and advan-
tageous match presenting itself, and being recommended to him by the desires of his noble friends, he
consented to the motion taking to wife one of the
sisters of the right honourable the Viscount Baltin-
glass, by whom he hath issue one only son, now
six years old, a very hopeful youth, having had
by his former wife another son of the age of 21
years or thereabouts, now a hopeful student in
Cambridge. In the year 1655 when the usurping
Protector had published an interdict against ecclesiastical persons, schoolmasters, and others who had
adhered to his late sacred Majesty, or assisted the

present, whereby they were prohibited to perform
any ministerial office, teach school, etc., upon several
pains and forfeitures, the good doctor forbore not to
preach as he did before. The convincing power
either of his doctrine or his worth defending and keeping him out of the hands of that unreasonable man.

This unchristian barbarous cruelty of that trial,
sorely afflicted the good doctor in his first apprehensions of it, though after a little consultation and
the encouragement of friends, and the strong persuasions of his own conscience, he came to a resolution
to do his duty as a minister of Christ, and leave the
issue to God. But he did not only look upon this
prohibition, in general, as a severe punishment
inflicted upon the nation by removing their teachers
into corners, nay remote corners of the world if they
disobeyed that edict, but in particular (at first view
of it) as some punishment or infliction on himself, as
if God had refused him and laid him aside as not fit
to serve Him, and this he referred to his former
remissness in the discharge of that high function
whereunto he was separated and called. And now
did he superabundantly exercise that grace of charity,
to all persons distressed and ruined by this sad
occasion : what his own small estate could not do he
helped out by exhorting and persuading all men of

his acquaintance or congregation (for so was the Church of England reduced, even in that to the form of that schism that ruined it,) or select auditory, so that what by his powerful example, and as strong persuasions, he did minister effectually to their relief. Not to omit one particular charitable office of this doctor to the same kind of sufferers, from the expiration of the war, he constantly retained one that had been a captain in the royal army, and whose fortunes and condition could neither keep him according to that degree, nor sustain nor relieve him in any other. This the good doctor did out of a loyal and honourable sense of such persons' sufferings and contempts far unworthy their cause or their desert, and did therefore allow him £10 yearly besides diet and lodging till the captain died. About this time the doctor became chaplain to the right honourable [George] Lord Berkeley, having quitted Waltham, in lieu whereof, this lord presented him with the living of Cranford in Middlesex (where his body is now deposited :) how infinitely well beloved he was there needs not be added to those accumulations of respect he found everywhere, for fear especially of resuscitating the recent grief of those parishioners for his late lamented loss.

He was a little before wooed also to accept of a

living at —— in Essex, which for some respects he
owed the patron and to employ that rich talent with
which God had so bountifully trusted him, he undertook and piously there continued his labours till his
settlement in London.

In the interim came out a book of Dr. Heylin's
called *Animadversions upon Mr. Fuller's Ecclesiastical
History*, wherein somewhat tartly (though with that
judicious learning for which that doctor is most deservedly honoured) he taxed that book of some errors,
etc. To this the doctor replied by a book styled *The
appeal of injured innocence to the learned and ingenious
reader*. Being a very modest but most rational and
polite defence to the aforesaid exceptions against that
elaborate piece. The dispute and controversy was soon
ended, and the oil the doctor bestowed on this labour
being poured into the fresh wound of this quarrel did
so assuage the heat of the contest that it was soon
healed into a perfect amicable closure and unusual en-
dearment. Indeed the grace that was supereminent in
the good doctor was charity, both in giving and for-
giving, as he had laboured during our civil broils after
peace. So when that could not through our sins be attained, did he with the same earnestness press the duty
of love, especially among brethren of the same afflicted
and too much already divided church, and therefore

was most exemplary in keeping the band of it himself,
though in a matter that most nearly concerned his
credit and fame, the chiefest worldly thing he studied
and intended. This constrained retrospection of the
doctor to secure and assist the far advanced strength
of his foremost works, did a little retard and impede
the arrear of his labours, which consisted of the flower
and choice of all his abilities and wherein his *Worthies*
were placed. Howbeit this proved but a halt, to those
encumbrances and difficulties, which he had all along
before met, and soon set that book on foot again.
This was the last remora to it, the doctor going on a
smooth swift pace, while all things else were retro-
grade in the kingdom, through the tyrannical plots
and stratagems of the usurper Cromwell, so as towards
the beginning of that *mirabilis annus* 1660 he had it
ready for the press, to which as soon as the wonder
of his majesty's restitution was over (in the thankful
contemplation whereof the good doctor was so piously
fixed, as nothing else might presume to intrude upon
his raised gladded spirit) he brought it, taking the
auspicia of that happy and famous juncture of time
for the commencement of this everlasting monument
of himself as well as all other English noble deceased
persons. A while before to complete the doctor's contentment as to his ministry also, he was invited to his

former lecturer's place in the Savoy, who even from
his departure had suffered under an insufficient or
disloyal and malicious clergy, and therefore stood in
need of an able and dutiful son of the Church to
reduce and lead them in the right way and the old
paths. For this people (his ancient flock) the doctor
had always a more especial respect and kindness,
which was the rather heightened in him out of a compassion to their state and condition. Nor did he
more tenderly affect them than they universally
respect him, receiving him (as indeed he was) as an
angel of God, sent to minister unto them heavenly
things, in exchange whereof they freely gave him their
hearts and hands.

The doctor through the injury and iniquity of the
times, had for near twenty years been barred of all
the profits of his prebendaryship of Salisbury (of
which before) but upon the return of the king, those
revenues and possessions so sacrilegiously alienated
from the church reverted also to their rightful pro-
prietors. This accession and additional help did very
much encourage the doctor in the carrying on of his
book, which being large would require an able purse
to go through with, and he was very solicitous, (often
presaging he should not live to see it finished though
satisfied of his present healthy constitution) to have it

done out of hand, to which purpose part of the money accruing to him from his Salisbury prebendaryship was designed. He therefore hastened his book with all expidition, and whereas he had intended to continue it but till 1659, and had therefore writ it in such language as those times of usurpation (during the most part of which it was compiled) would suffer such a subject and concerning matter to be dressed in, he now reviewed it over, giving truth, and his own most excellent fancy their proper becoming ornaments, scope, and clearness. But neither the elevation of the usurpers, nor the depression of the royalists, and the *vice versa* of it, did ever incline or sway him to additions, intercalations, or expunctions of persons whom he had recommended to the world for *Worthies*, no such thing as a Pym or Protector whom the mad world cried up for brave. Drops of compassionate tears they did force from him, but his resolute ink was not to be stained by their black actions. A pen full of such would serve to blot out the whole roll of fame. This constancy of the doctor's to his first model and main of his design doth most evidently argue his firm persuasion and belief of the reviving of the royal cause, since he wrote the most part during those improbable times of any restitutions, and he had very ill consulted his own advantage, if he had not well con-

sulted the oracles of God. As the last felicity of this
doctor's life, he was made chaplain in extraordinary
to his Majesty, being also in a well grounded expectation of some present further advancement; but here
death stepped in, and drew the curtain betwixt him
and his succeeding ecclesiastical dignities. And would
a curtain were drawn here too, that the said remainder
of this task were enjoined to the last trump, when we
shall know likewise wherefore God was so pleased to
take him from us, and be satisfied with His providence.
Pity the envious should find such an imperfection in
him as death, pity the grateful should mourn so long
and so much for the loss of him and his most incom-
parable gifts and endowments without any redress;
—but *infandos Fullere jubes renovare dolores*—we must
continue our discourse though upon a discontinued
subject, and write the much deplored death of doctor
Fuller.

Having in August returned from Salisbury, whither
he went to settle and let his revenue as prebend of
that deanery, he returned to his charge at London. It
was a very sickly time in the country, the distempers
most rife were feverish agues, the disease of which
our doctor died, and therefore it was judged, that he
had brought the infection of his disease thence, which
broke out violently upon him soon after his return,

(doctor Nicholas the reverend dean of Paul's dying
near the same time upon his coming from the same
place), for being desired to preach a marriage sermon
on Sunday the twelfth of August, for a kinsman of his,
who was to be wedded the day after, the good doctor
lovingly undertook it. But on that Sunday dinner
felt himself very much indisposed, complaining of a
dizziness in his head, whereupon his son intreated him
that he would go and lie down on bed, and forbear
preaching that afternoon, informing him how dangerous
those symptoms were, but the doctor would not be
persuaded, but to church he would go and perform his
promise to his friend, saying "he had gone up often
into the pulpit sick, but always came well down again,
and he hoped he should do as well now through God's
strengthening grace."

Being in the pulpit, he found himself very ill, so
that he was apprehensive of the danger, and therefore
before his prayer addressed himself thus to his congregation. "I find myself very ill, but I am resolved
by the grace of God to preach this sermon to you
here, though it be my last." A sad presage and more
sadly verified. He proceeded in his prayer and sermon
very perfectly till in the middle (never using himself
to notes other than the beginning word of each head
or division) he began to falter, but not so much out

but that he quickly recollected himself, and very pertinently concluded. After he had awhile sat down, he was not able to rise again, but was fain to be led down the pulpit stairs by two men into the reading place. He had promised also to christen a child (of a very good friend of his) then in the church, and the parent did earnestly importune him to do it, and the good doctor was as willing as he desiring, but the doctor's son showing him the extreme danger there was of his father, he desisted from his request. Much ado there was to persuade the doctor to go home in a sedan, he saying still he should be well by and by, and would go along with them, but at last finding himself worse and worse he yielded to go but not to his old lodgings (which were convenient for him in the Savoy) but to his new one in Covent-Garden. Being come thither they had him to bed and presently sent for doctor Scarborough but he being in the country doctor Charlton came, who with the exactest skill and care possible, addressed himself to the recovery of the good doctor. The disease was judged by him to be a violent malignant fever, such as then raged everywhere, and was better known by the name of the new disease, which like a plague had swept away a multitude of people throughout the kingdom. Therefore phlebotomy was directed and

some twenty ounces of blood taken from him, and yet
nevertheless the paroxysms continued, having totally
bereft the doctor of all sense, so much as to give any
the least account of his condition, the physician's art
being at a loss and not able to advise any further
against the unsuperable violence and force of the distemper. Yet in this sad and oppressed condition,
some comfortable signs and assurances were given
by the good doctor by his frequent lifting up his
hands and his eyes, which devotion ended in folding
of his arms, and sighs fetched questionless from a
perfect contrition for this life and from an earnest
desire after, and hope of that to come. On Tuesday
August 14, the good doctor gave sad symptoms of a
prevailing disease, and Dr. Charlton despaired of
his recovery, his fever being so fierce and pertinacious
and which resisted all remedies. As was said almost
from the very first decumbency which was near as
soon as he was ill, his senses were seized and surprised
with little or no remission of the distemper, which
caused him to talk sometimes, but of nothing more
frequently than his books, calling for pen and ink,
and telling his sorrowful attendants that by and by
he should be well and would write it out . . etc.

But on Wednesday noon, the presages of a dislodg-
ing soul were apparent in him, for nature being over-

d

powered the vitals burnt up by such a continual heat
his lamp of life began to decay, his fever and strength
abating together, so that it pleased God to restore to
him the use of the faculties of his soul, which he very
devoutly and thankfully employed in a christian pre-
paration for death, earnestly imploring the prayers of
some of his reverend brethren with him, who then
were sorrowful visitors of him in these his last agonies,
which accordingly was performed, the good doctor
with all the intentness of piety joining with them, and
recommending himself with all humble thankfulness
and submission to God's welcome providence. Nay
so highly was he affected with God's pleasure concerning him, that he could not endure any person to weep
or cry, but would earnestly desire them to refrain,
highly extolling and preferring his condition as a
translation to a blessed eternity. Nor would he therefore endure to hear anything of the world or worldly
matters, for the settling and disposition whereof he
had before made no provision, and who was desired
by some to give some present direction, for the better
accommodating the several concerns of his family.
But the doctor totally rejected any thoughts of those
matters, having his mind engaged and prepossessed
with things of ravishing and transcendent excellencies.
Even his beloved book, aforesaid, the darling of his

soul, was totally neglected not a syllable dropping
from him in reference to the perfecting and finishing
thereof which he had brought so near to the birth.
Nothing but heaven and the perfections thereof,
the consummations of grace in glory, must fill up the
room of his capacious soul, which now was flitting and
ready to take wing to those mansions of bliss.   For
on Thursday morning August 16, 1661, this reverend
and painful minister of Christ Jesus, having finished
his course, and run the race that was set before him,
and fought a good fight, breathed out his wearied
spirit into the hands of his Redeemer to his own everlasting fruition and consolation, but to the irreparable
loss and very exceeding sorrow of all men, to whom
religion, piety, virtue and super-eminent learning were
ever acceptable.   And what ever the present envious
world may think, unprejudiced posterity will un-
doubtedly erect him a shrine, and pay him those *justa*
of honour and fame which to his memory most duly
and rightly do belong.

    After he had laid a while dead, an eruption of blood
burst from his temples which was conjectured to have
been long settled there, through too much study in
the methodizing and completing those various pieces
in his *Worthies General* of which he was prophetically
afraid he should never live to see the finishing.

He was buried at the desire and at the cost of the
right honourable his noble patron the lord Berkeley
at his parish of Cranford in Middlesex, in the chancel
of the said church, and attended thither by at least
two hundred of his brethren of the ministry, such
a solemn assembly being scarce to be paralleled,
where the reverend dean of Rochester, Dr. Hardy,
preached his funeral sermon, being a very elegant and
extraordinary pathetical deploration of so great a loss,
which hath not yet (though it is hoped and much
desired may) passed the press, to which learned piece
with all humble submission, be referred the praises
and commendations of this deceased doctor, being
thereby so excellently well transmitted to his everlasting rest.

Though we have now brought this venerable doctor
to his repository, and laid him in his silent grave, yet
there remain some further offices due to his yet speaking virtues and graces, the smooth and fair track
whereof could not be so well insisted on in the fore-
going considerations of him, as in *via*, and that so sale-
brose and difficult by the unevenness and asperity of
the times he lived in; but do now orderly lead us
without any diversion, as he is in glory to the pursuit
of his fame and memory.   In tendency whereunto it

is requisite to enliven that portrait of him prefixed
to this manual, with some of those natural graces
which were unexpressible in him by the pencil, withal
to shew what a convenient habitation learning and
virtue had chosen, in which nothing could be complained of and faulted, but that they took it for so
short a term. He was of stature somewhat tall,
exceeding the mean, with a proportionable bigness to
become it, but no way inclining to corpulency. Of
an exact straightness of the whole body, and a perfect
symmetry in every part thereof. He was of a sanguine constitution, which beautified his face with a
pleasant ruddiness, but of so grave and serious an
aspect, that it awed and discountenanced the smiling
attracts of that complexion. His head adorned with
a comely light coloured hair, which was so by nature
exactly curled (an ornament enough of itself in this
age, to denominate a handsome person, and wherefore
all skill and art is used) but not suffered to overgrow
to any length unseeming his modesty and profession.
His gait and walking was very upright and graceful,
becoming his well shapen bulk, approaching something near to that we term majestical, but that the
doctor was so well known to be void of any affectation
or pride. Nay so regardless was he of himself in his
garb and raiment, in which no doubt his vanity would

have appeared, as well as in his stately pace, that it
was with some trouble to himself to be either neat
or decent, it mattered not for the outside while
he thought himself never too curious and nice in the
dresses of his mind. Very careless also he was to
seeming inurbanity in the modes of courtship and
demeanour, disporting himself much according to the
old English guise which for its ease and simplicity
suited very well with the doctor, whose time was
designed for more elaborate business, and whose
motto might have been sincerity.

As unobservant he was of persons unless business
with them, or his concerns pointed them out and
adverted him, seeing and discerning were two things ;
often in several places hath he met with gentlemen of
his nearest and greatest acquaintance at a full ren-
counter and stop, whom he hath endeavoured to
pass by, not knowing, that is to say, not minding of
them, till rectified and recalled by their familiar com-
pellations.

This will not (it may be presumed) and justly
cannot be imputed unto any indisposedness and
unaptness of his nature, which was so far from rude
and untractable that it may be confidently averred,
he was the most complacent person in the nation, as
his converse and writings, with such a freedom of

discourse and quick jocundity of style, do sufficiently
evince. He was a perfect walking library, and those
that would find delight in him must turn him, he was
to be diverted from his present purpose with some
urgency, and when once unfixed and unbent, his
mind freed from the incumbency of his study, no
man could be more agreeable to civil and serious
mirth, which limits his most heightened fancy never
transgressed.

He had the happiness of a very honourable and
that very numerous acquaintance, so that he was no
way undisciplined in the arts of civility, yet he continued *semper idem* which constancy made him always
acceptable to them.   At his diet he was very sparing
and temperate, but yet he allowed himself the repasts
and refreshings of two meals a day, but no lover of
dainties, or the inventions of cookery; solid meats
better fitting his strength of constitution, but from
drink very much abstemious, which questionless was
the cause of that uninterrupted health he enjoyed till
this his first and last sickness, of which felicity as he
himself was partly the cause of by his exactness in
eating and drinking, so did he the more dread the
sudden infliction of any disease or other violence of
nature, fearing this his care might amount to a
presumption in the eyes of the Great Disposer

of all things, and so it pleased God it should happen.

But his great abstinence of all was from sleep, and strange it was that one of such a fleshly and sanguine composition could over watch so many heavy propense inclinations to rest. For this in some sort he was beholden to his care in diet aforesaid, (the full vapours of a repletion in the stomach ascending to the brain, causing that usual drowsiness we see in many), but most especially to his continual custom, use, and practise, which had so subdued his nature, that it was wholly governed by his active and industrious mind.

And yet this is a further wonder : he did scarcely allow himself from his first degree in the University any recreation or easy exercise, no not so much as walking, but very rare and seldom, and that not upon his own choice, but as being compelled by friendly, yet forcible invitations, till such time as the war posted him from place to place, and after that his constant attendance on the press in the edition of his books, when was a question which went the fastest, his head or his feet ; so that in effect he was a very stranger if not an enemy to all pleasure. Riding was the most pleasant because his necessary convenience, the doctor's occasions especially his last work re-

quiring travel, to which he had so accustomed himself, so that this diversion (like princes' banquets only
to be looked upon by them not tasted of) was rather
made such, than enjoyed by him. So that if there
were any felicity or delight, which he can be truly
said to have had, it was either in his relations, or in
his works. As to his relations certainly no man was
more a tender, more indulgent a husband and a
father. His conjugal love in both matches being
equally blessed with the same issue, kept a constant
tenour in both marriages, which he so improved, that
the harmony of his affections stilled all discord and
charmed the noise of passion.

Towards the education of his children he was
exceeding careful, allowing them anything conducing
to that end beyond the present measure of his estate,
which is well hoped will be returned to the memory
of so good a father in their early imitation of him in
all those good qualities and literature to which they
have now such a hereditary claim. As to his books
which we usually call the issue of the brain, he was
more than fond, totally abandoning and forsaking all
things to follow them. And yet if correction and
severity (so this may be allowed the gravity of the
subject) be also the signs of love, a stricter and more
careful hand was never used. True it is they did not

grow up without some errors like the tares, nor can the most refined pieces of any of his antagonists boast of perfection. He that goes an unknown and beaten track in a dubious way, though he may have good directions, yet if in the journey he chance to stray cannot well be blamed, they have perchance ploughed with his heifer and been beholden to those authorities (for their exceptions) which he first gave light to.

To his neighbours and friends he behaved himself with that cheerfulness and plainness of affection and respect as deservedly gained him their highest esteem from the meanest to the highest. He omitted nothing what to him belonged to his station, either in a familiar correspondency or necessary visits ; never suffering entreaties of that which either was his duty, or in his power to perform. The quickness of his apprehension helped by a good nature presently suggested unto him (without putting them to the trouble of an *innuendo*) what their several affairs required, in which he would spare no pains, insomuch that it was a piece of absolute prudence to rely upon his advice and assistance. In a word, to his superiors he was dutifully respectful without ceremony or officiousness, to his equals he was discreetly respectful, without neglect or unsociableness, and to his inferiors (whom indeed

he judged christianly none to be) civilly respectful
without pride or disdain. But all these so eminent
virtues, and so sublimed in him, were but as foils to
those excellent gifts wherewith God had endued his
intellectuals. He had a memory of that vast comprehensiveness, that is deservedly known for the first
inventor of that noble art, whereof having left behind
him no rules, or directions save only what fell from
him in discourse, no further account can be given,
but a relation of some very rare experiments of it
made by him. He undertook once in passing to
and fro from Temple bar to the furthest conduit in
Cheapside, at his return again, to tell every sign,
as they stood in order, on both sides of the way,
repeating them either backward or forward, as they
should choose, which he exactly did, not missing
or misplacing one, to the admiration of those that
heard him. The like also would he do in words of
different languages, and of hard and difficult prolation
to any number whatever, but that which was most
strange and very rare in him, was his way of writing,
which something like the Chinese was from the top of
the page to the bottom ; the manner thus. He would
write near the margin the first words of every line
down to the foot of the paper, then would he beginning at the head again, fill up every one of these lines

which without any interlineations or spaces, but with
the full and equal length, would so adjust the sense
and matter, and so aptly connex and conjoin the ends
and beginnings of the said lines, that he could not do
it better as he hath said, if he had writ all out in a
continuation. The treasury of this happy memory
was a very great advantage to his preaching, but
being assisted with as rich invention and extraordinary
reading did absolutely complete him for the pulpit.
His great stores both of school and case divinity,
both of history, and philosophy, of arts, and tongues,
his converse in the Scriptures, the fathers, and humane
writings had so abundantly furnished him that without the other additaments he had been very eminent
among his function. Now all so happily met together,
such a constellation could portend no less than some
wonder of men who should be famous in his generation. Not to omit to this purpose (however to the
first intuition it may seem to the reverend and graver
divines a precipitancy and a venturous rashness in
any man with such unprovidedness to step into the
pulpit) that this venerable doctor upon some sudden
emergent occasions upon two hours warning, and
upon a subject of his friends choice which was knotty,
and very difficult, hath performed the task enjoined
him with much accurateness; such his art of method, be-

sides that his understanding was strangely opened, for
the unlocking and opening of Scriptures, which he would
do very genuinely and evidently, and then embellish
his explication with curious variety of expression.

For his ordinary manner of teaching, it was in some
kind different from the usual preacher's method of most
ministers in those times, for he seldom made any
excursions into the handling of common places, or
drew his subject matter out at length by any pro-
lixely continued discourse. But the main frame of
his public sermons, if not wholly consisting (after some
brief and genuine resolution of the context and
explication of the terms where need required, of notes
and observations with much variety and great dexterity
drawn immediately from the text, and naturally without constraint issuing or flowing either from the main
body, or from the several parts of it, with some useful
applications annexed thereunto ; which though either
of them long insisted upon yet were wont with that
vivacity to be propounded and pressed by him as
well might, and oft did pierce deep into the hearts of
his hearers, and not only rectify and clear their judgments but have a powerful work also upon their
affections. Nor was it his manner to quote many
Scriptures, finding it troublesome to himself and
supposing it would be so to his auditors also; besides

deeming it the less needful in regard that his observations being grounded immediately on the Scripture
he handled, and by necessary consequence thence
deduced, seemed to receive proof sufficient from it.
A constant form of prayer he used, as in his family,
so in his public ministry ; only varying or adding upon
special occasions, as occurrences intervening required ;
because not only hesitation (which the good doctor
for all his strength of memory and invention was
afraid of before so awful a presence as the Majesty of
Heaven) was in prayer more offensive than other
discourse, but because such excursions in that duty in
the extempore way were become the idol of the
multitude.   In his *Mixt Contemplations* read these
words : "Let such new practises as are to be brought
into our church, be, for a time, candidates and pro-
bationers on their good behaviour, to see how the
temper of people will fit them, and they fadge with it
before they be publicly enjoined.   Let them be like
Saint Paul's deacons 1 Tim. 3, *first be proved* then be
used, if found blameless.   I cannot therefore but
commend the discretion of such statesmen, who knowing the directory to be but a stranger, and considering
the great inclination the generality of our nation had
to the Common Prayer, made their temporary act to
stand in force but for three years."   He could as well

declare his mind and errand, and of all others likewise, with as much plainness, clearness, and (which is more) reverence, as any of those who cried up the Spirit, and their own way in opposition to the laws and the judgment of antiquity, so to take the people with their new fangled words, and licentious easiness of discoursing with God Almighty, whose attributes they squared to their petitions, that it be not said, wills. As he was an enemy to the inventions of men, obtruded upon the Blessed Spirit in that irreverend and profane manner of praying and revelation; so was he likewise on the other side a professed and avowed adversary to the mass, and traditions, which caused him no little slander and obloquy. But the spirit of this pious doctor was exceedingly stirred in him against all popish insinuators; because he was too sensible that through the mad zeal of the vulgar, whom they had by jesuitical practices inflamed, the house of God in these kingdoms was set in combustion. Therefore with much prudence, courage, and boldness, did he everywhere in his books as occasion offered, unmask the deceits and designs, resist and curb the pride, convince and lay open the errors of the Church of Rome : though he never wrote anything particularly by way of controversy against it, because as he said there is no end of it : and more than sufficient had already been wrote ; if any ingenuity had been in the adherents of that see, to have submitted to the truth. Nor was there ever any of that religion who were so hardy as to challenge or tax the doctor, but obliquely, for anything wherewith he had charged them, either of apostacy, heresy, or manifest idolatry, their abuse of antiquity in their rasures and additions, which did very often occur to him in most of his books, from which they were sure to hear of them to the purpose. It much rejoiced the Roman party when that misunderstanding happened betwixt doctor Heylin and himself about his Ecclesiastical History though they caught no fish in those troubled waters while they tossed of their proud billows forward and backward, the protestant cause was safely anchored and moored between them.

And as he never had occasion to engage in any polemical discourse with any of that party ; so in these miserable bandyings of our late unhappy times did he always refrain from stickling in any side, though it was sufficiently known how firmly grounded and addict to the true protestant religion, in opposition to the innovations of presbytery and the schism of independency against whom also he had a zeal, but allayed with a greater compassion, than to the papist, distinguishing betwixt the seducers and the seduced, whom notwithstanding he did very severely deal withal in his writings; one instance whereof take in his *Mixt Contemplations.* "I am sad, that I may add with too much truth, that one man will at last be divided in himself, distracted often betwixt many opinions; that what is reported of Tostatus lying on his death bed, *In multitudine controversiarum non habuit quod crederet,* amongst the multitude of persuasions, through which he had passed, he knew not where to cast anchor and fix himself at last." So that he may be said to have been a right-handed enemy to the stubborn Romanist and a left-handed one to the cunning sectary.

He was wont to call those controversies concerning episcopacy, and the new invented arguments against the church of England with the answers and refutations thereof, ημερόβια, things of a day's life and of no permanency, the church being built upon a rock, as no storms could shake or move it, so needed it not any defences of art or learning. Being of the same mind with Sir Henry Wootton *disputandi pruritus, scabies ecclesiæ.* He was wholly conversant during the broils and dissensions of the clergy in the thoughts and considerations of that text: *Let your moderation be known to all men,* on which place he once preached a while before his majesty's restitution to a very great auditory, little imagining the subsequent words, *For the Lord is at hand,* were so near the fulfilling in the merciful visitations of God towards these miserable nations. In this he was the same still, but more solicitous in the glimmering of that happy revolution ; when he plainly saw how indispensably necessary the mutual condescensions of all parties were to the establishment and consolidating of peace (*Mixt Contemplations* to this purpose again) " Peace in our land, like St. Paul at Athens betwixt to sects of philosophers, is now like to be encountered with two such opposite parties such as are for the liberties of a Commonwealth, and such as are for an absolute Monarchy in the full length thereof. But I hope neither of them, both are so considerable in their number, parts and influences on the people; but that the moderate party advocates for peace will prevail for the settling thereof, *ibidem.* The episcopal party doth desire and expect that the presbyterian should remit of his rigidness in order to an expedient between them, the presbyterians require that the episcopal side abate of their authority to advance an accommodation. But some on both sides are so wedded to their wilfulness, stand so stiff on their judgments, are so hot and high in their passions, they will not part with the least punctilio in their opinions and practices. Such men's

judgments cannot pretend to the exactness of the
Gibeonites, Judg. xx. 16, that they hit the mark of an
hair's breadth and fail not, yet will they not abate an
hair's breadth in order to unity ; they will take all,
but tender nothing ; make motions with their mouths,
but none with their feet for peace, not stirring a step
towards it. . . . Oh that we could see some proffers
and performances of condescension on either side, and
then let others who remain obstinate, be branded with
Phazes, Gen. xxxviii. 29, *the breach be upon them.*"

Thus the good doctor's bent and resolutions were for
a fair and mutual compliance out of a tender jealousy
of this divided church, seeing other men resolved
indeed into an obstinate resistance and adherence
to their opinions, who would rather rashly cut the
Gordian knot of union and concord, to fulfil the
doubtful oracles of their own judgment, than leisurely
and with patience endeavour the untying of it, which
would set the Church of God at perfect liberty and
release it from the violence of prejudiced and cap-
tived reason.

How much this lay upon his spirit, being the
Benjamin of his love, above all other duties and
necessities in a christian conversation, or government, may seem further tedious to relate ; but because
it is so genuine a trait of his elegant pen, and so

like him, it is hoped that this excellent feature copied
here in this rude transcript of him may be of delight
(amidst the mass and undigestedness of these collections,) to the curious reader. "In my father's
time there was a Fellow of Trinity College in Cambridge, a native of Carleton in Leicestershire, where
the people through some occult cause are troubled
with a wharling in their throats so that they cannot
plainly pronounce the letter R. This scholar, being
conscious of his infirmity, made a Latin oration of the
usual expected length, without an R therein, and yet
did he not only select words fit for his easy pro-
nunciation, but also as pure and expressive for signi-
fication, to shew that these men might speak without
being beholden to the dog's letter. . . . Our English
pulpits for these last eighteen years, have had in
them too much caninal anger vented by snapping
and snarling spirits on both sides. *But if you bite and
devour one another*, saith the Apostle, Gal. v. 15, *take
heed ye be not devoured one of another.* Think not our
sermons must be silent if not satirical, as if divinity
did not afford smooth subjects enough to be season-
ably insisted on in this juncture of time. Let us try
our skill, whether we cannot preach without any dog
letter or biting word; the art is half learned by in-
tending, and wholly by serious endeavouring of it. . .

I am sure that such soft sermons will be more easy
for the tongue of the preacher in pronouncing them;
less grating to the ears of pious persons that hear
them; and most edifying to the heart of both speaker
and hearer . . again and for all. . . Oh may the state
be pleased so far to reflect on this Isaac as to settle
the inheritance on him. Let protestant religion be only
countenanced by law, be owned and acknowledged
for the received religion of the nation. As for other
sects, the sons of Keturah, we grudge not that gifts
be bestowed on them. Let them have a toleration
(and that I assure you is a great gift indeed) and be
permitted peaceably, but privately to enjoy their
consciences, both in opinions and practices; such
favour may safely, not to say ought, justly be afforded
unto them, so long as they continue peaceably in our
Israel and not disturb the state." This is the rather
inserted both for the catelousness of the expression
he used, and which those times required; and by
which discreet and amicable way our differences
and breaches were likeliest to be made up. The disguises of words to the undeceiving of a misled
people into the right way of their felicity, who had
all along been driven with speeches, and such like
parliament oratory, being the facilest method of introducing that peace which by the same arts was

violated. Storms begin from, and end in calms, the
gentle breathings of soft and temperate spirits commencing the outrages of other men's violent passions,
and terminating and stopping their fury.

This was a charitable and also a reasonable and
political design of the doctor's, very well applied in
the crisis of that distemper, whose acute pains in the
stripping of those people of their illegal possessions
and purchases, (though in time they might and would
naturally and centrally return to their just owners)
were to be alleviated and eased by some healing
balsam, not to be lanced and exasperated by the
sharp and keen incisions of invectives and exproba-
tions, those tumours and swellings of usurped estates
being better to be laid by lenitives and suppling oils,
than to be eaten away by corrosives, or cut off by
cruel instruments. This policy more eminent in
illustrious persons (though not the charity of the
good doctor) God succeeded in that juncture of time
by amusing the most considerable persons, as well
as the generality of the engaged rebellious faction
and party, into a supineness or (which was the
greater work of Providence that doth commonly go
by a method) confident reliance on the king's grace
and kindness. Those who would not trust his blessed
father though under confirmation of his royal seal and

word, to be further strengthened by their own authority in parliament, were quiet and contented in the only bare · expectation what his royal son would promise them.   But the doctor's charity as before, though so extensive, was far overreached by that liberty of conscience, which interest and self will and the pride of schism stretched beyond all convenient or reasonable limits : his condescensions to such as went by the name of tender christians signifying no more than some acts of grace and pardon lately passed, so that all the good the doctor did in that respect was to himself, the benefit of that love and charity being returned and multiplied on him to his everlasting comfort.   But what the measure of his charity could not fulfil, was made up in his piety and constant intercession, that they might prove such, as he in his best thoughts had wished them.   He was most earnest in this duty of prayer, and his often accesses to that mercy seat had made it a place of acquaintance and free reception.   As his study importuned him at very unreasonable hours, so it opportuned his devotions in the early and late sacrifices which he indispensably and firstly offered to the God of heaven, a phrase for its comprehensiveness of the Divine Majesty in the glory and perfection of it above all other his creatures, very familiar and usual

with the doctor by way of emphasis, or reverend
instance. If it may pass here without any rigid
adversion a very excellent passage of the doctor's
(in the beginning of the anarchy under a Commonwealth) would seek admittance, having relation to this
duty in hand. Soon after the king's death he preached
in a church near London, and a person then in great
power (now levelled with his fellows) was present at
the sermon, in his prayer before which he said—" God
in his due time settle our nation on the true foundation thereof." The then great man demanded of
him what he meant by *the true foundation*? and he
answered, he was no lawyer nor statesman and therefore skill in such matters could not be expected from
him. But being pressed further to explain himself
whether thereby he did not intend the king, lords and
commons, he answered that it was a part of his
prayer to God, who had more knowledge than he
ignorance in all things, that he knew what was the
true foundation, and so remitted the factious querist
to God's wisdom and goodness. This was a kind of
his experiments in prayer, which were many and very
observable; God often answering his desires in kind,
and that immediately when he was in some distresses.
And God's providence in taking care and providing
for him in his whole course of life wrought in him a

firm resolution to depend upon him, in what condition soever he should be ; and he found that Providence, to continue in that tenour to his last end.
Indeed he was wholly possessed with a holy fear of,
and reliance in God, was conscionable in his private
duties, and in sanctifying the Sabbath ; being much
offended at its profanation by disorderly men, and
that both in reference to the glory of God, and the
scandal brought on the Church of England, as if it
allowed (as some have impudently affirmed) such
wicked licentiousness.   For his own particular, very
few Sundays there were in the year in which he
preached not twice : besides the duties performed
in his own house or in his attendance on those noble
persons to whom successively he was chaplain.   So
that if he had not been helped by a more than
officious memory which devoured all the books he
read, and digested them to easy nutriment, that supplied all the parts and the whole body of his learning,
for his service and furtherance of his labours ; it had
been impossible but that the duties he performed
as a divine, must have hindered and jostled out those
his happy productions as a most complete historian.
Which study being tied to the series and catenation
of time and truth, could ill brook or break through
those avocations, though no doubt it thrived the

better under the kindly influence of his devotion. It will make it also the less wonder why a man of so great merit and such conspicuous worth, should never arrive to any eminent honour and dignity, or church revenue, save that of prebend of Salisbury, being also of competent age to become the gravity of such preferments; for he could not afford to seek great matters for himself who designed his all for the public good and the concerns of his precious soul. Questionless he could not have wanted friends to his advancement, if he would have pursued such ends; who would have been as great furtherers of himself out of a particular affection (which is always ambitious of laying such obligations upon virtue) to his person, as they had assisted him in his works and labours. He was reward and recompense enough to himself, and for his fame and glory certainly he computed it the best way; 'tis the jewel that graces the ring, not so contrary. High places are levelled in death, and crumble into dust, leaving no impression of those that possessed them, and are only retrievable to posterity by some excellent portraits of their nobler part; wherein it will on all hands be confessed, the doctor hath absolutely drawn himself beyond the most excellent counterfeit of art, and which shall outlive all addition of monument and outflourish the

pomp of the most lasting sepulchral glory. But had
the worthy doctor but some longer while survived,
to the fruition of that quiet and settlement of the
church, of which by God's goodness and favour we
have so full a prospect, and that the crowd of suitors
to ecclesiastical promotions had left thronging and
importuning their great friends, to the stifling and
smothering of modest merit, it may be presumed the
royal bounty would favourably have reflected on, and
respected, that worth of the doctor (which was so
little set by and regarded of himself in his contented
obscurity) by a convenient placing and raising of
that light to some higher orb, from whence he should
have dilated and dispensed his salutiferous rays and
influences. Some little time after his death his course
would have come to have preached before his majesty,
for which the doctor made preparations, and that
most probably would have proved a fit opportunity
for notifying himself to the king, whose most judicious and exact observation the remarks of the
doctor would have happily suited. This honour was
designed him before by a right noble lord in whose
retinue as chaplain he went over to the Hague, at the
reduction of his majesty into these his kingdoms.
But the haste and dispatch which that great affair
required in the necessity of the king's presence here

afforded him not the effect of that honourable intendment, but what he was disappointed of here, is fully
attained by his happy appearance before the King of
Kings, to praise and magnify Him and to sing Halle-
lujahs for ever.   So adieu to that glory of the doctor,
which is incommunicable with the world.   And *ave*
and all prosperity be to those his remains, which he
hath to the general advantage of learning and piety
most liberally imparted.

Too customary were it to recite the several kinds
and sorts of honourable epithets which his equal
readers have fixed on him, but this under favour may
be assigned peculiarly to him, that no man performed
any thing of such difficulty as his undertakings with
that delight and profit which were as the gemelli and
twins of his hard labour, and superfetation of wit, not
distinguishable but by the thread of his own art which
clued men into their several and distinct apartments.
And so impertinent it will be to engage further in a
particular account of his books, whose sure and per-
petual duration needs not the minutes of this biography,
especially that his ultimate piece and partly post-
humous, (his often mentioned book *The Worthies
General of England*) whose design was drawn by
eternity commencing from them (before) unknown
originals, and leading into an ocean of new discoveries,

and may some happy as hardy pen attempt the continuation.

The names of his other books having had their due reception need no other mention to posterity than what you have in this ensuing catalogue.

BOOKS OF DR. FULLER.

POEMS.

Hainousnesse of sinne,
Heavy punishment, and
Hearty Repentance. 8.

Holy war. 2. Folio.

Joseph's Party Coloured Coate, and Sermons on the Corinths. 4.

Holy State and prophane State. Folio.

Sermon of Reformation. 4.

Truth maintain'd, or an answer to Mr. Saltmarsh that writ against his Reformation Sermon. 4.

Inauguration Sermon preached at St. Westminster Abbey. 4.

A Sermon of Assurance. 4.

Good thoughts in bad times. 12.

Thoughts in worse times. 12.

Life of Andronicus. 8.

Cause and cure of a Wounded Conscience. 8.

Infants' Advocate. 8.

Pisgah sight of Palestine, or a description of the Holy Land. Folio with cuts.

Fuller's Triple Reconciler stating the controversies. 8.

Whether
 1. Ministers have an exclusive power of barring communicants from the Sacrament.
 2. Any person unordained may lawfully preach.
 3. The Lord's prayer ought not to be used by all Christians.

A Fast Sermon upon Innocents' Day. 4

Sermons on Matthew upon the Temptations. 8.

A Sermon of life out of death. 8.

Sermons on Ruth. 8.

Best Name on Earth.   8.

Another 8 of Sermons.

Speeches of the Beast and Flowers.   8.

Church History of Brittaine.   Folio.

Mixt Contemplations in these times.   Folio.

Lives of several Modern Divines in the 4to. book by Fuller.   4.

The Appeale of Injured Innocence, to the Learned and Impartial Reader.

In Answer to some Animadversions of Dr. Heylin's on his Church History.

Fuller's History of the Worthies General of England.   *Now finisht.*   Folio.   An excellent piece.

Tract in Latine concerning the Church, not perfected by him.

These elegant pieces are the best epitaph can be inscribed on his tomb, where though he rest himself, yet shall the world never see an end of his labours.

FINIS.

THE HOLY STATE.

THE GOOD WIFE.

ST. PAUL first adviseth women to submit themselves to
their husbands, and then counselleth men to love their
wives.[1] And sure it was fitting that women should
first have their lesson given them, because it is hardest
to be learned, and therefore they need have the more
time to con it. For the same reason we first begin
with the character of a good wife.

She commandeth her husband in any equal matter
by constant obeying him. She never crosseth her
husband in the springtide of his anger, but stays till
it be ebbing water. And then mildly she argues the
matter, not so much to condemn him, as to acquit
herself. Surely men, contrary to iron, are worse to
be wrought upon when they are hot; and far more
tractable in cold blood.

---

[1] St. Paul to the Colossians iii. 18.

B

She keeps home if she has not her husband's company, or leave for her patent to go abroad : for the house is the woman's centre. It is written, *The sun ariseth—man goeth forth unto his work and to his labour until the evening :*[1] but it is said of the good woman, *She riseth while it is yet night :*[2] for man in the race of his work starts from the rising of the sun because his business is without doors, and not to be done without the light of heaven ; but the woman hath her work within the house, and therefore can make the sun rise by lighting of a candle.

Her clothes are rather comely than costly, and she makes plain cloth to be velvet by her handsome wearing it. She is none of our dainty dames, who love to appear in variety of suits every day new, as if a good gown, like a stratagem in war, were to be used but once : but our good wife sets up a sail according to the keel of her husband's estate ; and if of high parentage, she doth not so remember what she was by birth, that she forgets what she is by match.

Her husband's secrets she will not divulge. Especially she is careful to conceal his infirmities. If he be none of the wisest, she so orders it that he appears

---

[1] Psalm civ. 22.   [2] Prov. xxxi. 15.

on the public stage but seldom ; and then he hath conned his part so well, that he comes off with great applause.

In her husband's absence she is wife and deputy husband, which makes her double the files of her diligence. At his return he finds all things so well, that he wonders to see himself at home when he was abroad.

In her husband's sickness she feels more grief than she shows. Partly that she may not dishearten him ; and partly because she is not at leisure to seem so sorrowful, that she may be the more serviceable.

Her children though many in number are none in noise, steering them with a look whither she listeth. When they grow up, she teacheth them not pride but painfulness, making their hands to clothe their backs, and them to wear the livery of their own industry. She makes not her daughters gentlewomen before they be women, rather teaching them what they should pay to others, than receive from them.

The heaviest work of her servants she maketh light by orderly and seasonable enjoining it : wherefore her service is counted a preferment, and her teaching better than her wages.

THE GOOD HUSBAND.

Having formerly described a good wife; she will make a good husband, whose character we are now to present.

His love to his wife weakeneth not his ruling her, and his ruling lesseneth not his loving her. Wherefore he avoideth all fondness (a sick love, to be praised in none, and pardoned only in the newly married), whereby more have wilfully betrayed their command than ever lost it by their wives' rebellion.

He is constant to his wife, and confident of her. And sure where jealousy is the jailor, many break the prison, it opening more ways to wickedness than it stoppeth; so that where it findeth one it maketh ten dishonest.

He alloweth her meet maintenance, but measures it by his own estate: nor will he give less, nor can she ask more. Which allowance, if shorter than her deserts and his desire, he lengtheneth it out with his courteous carriage unto her.

That she may not entrench on his prerogative, he maintains her propriety in feminine affairs, yea therein he follows her advice. Causes that are properly of feminine cognizance he suffers her finally to decide, not so much as permitting an appeal to himself, that their jurisdictions may not interfere.

Knowing she is the weaker vessel, he bears with her infirmities. All hard using of her he detests, desiring therein to do not what may be lawful, but fitting.

He is careful that the wounds betwixt them take not air, and be publicly known. Jars concealed are half reconciled ; which if generally known, it is a double task to stop the breach at home, and men's mouths abroad. To this end he never publicly reproves her. An open reproof puts her to do penance before all that are present, after which many rather study revenge than reformation.

He beats not his wife after his death: one having a shrewd wife, yet loth to use her hardly in his life-time, awed her with telling her that he would beat her when he was dead, meaning that he would leave her no maintenance. This humour is unworthy a worthy man, who will endeavour to provide her a competent estate, yet he that impoverisheth his children to enrich his widow, destroys a quick hedge to make a dead one.

THE GOOD PARENT.

He sheweth his children in his own practice what to follow and imitate ; and in others, what to shun and avoid. For though *the words of the wise be as nails fastened by the masters of the assemblies,*[1] yet sure their examples are the hammer to drive them in to take the deeper hold. A father that whipped his son for swearing, and swore himself whilst he whipped him, did more harm by his example than good by his correction. Our wise parent both instructs his children in piety, and with correction blasts the first buds of profaneness in them. He that will not use the rod on his child, his child shall be used as a rod on him.

He observeth gavel-kind[2] in dividing his affections, though not his estate. He loves them (though he leaves them not) all alike. Indeed his main land he settles on the eldest : for where man takes away the birthright, God commonly takes away the blessing from a family. But as for his love, therein, like a well-drawn picture, he eyes all his children alike (if there be a parity of deserts), not parching one to drown another.

[1] Eccles. xii. 11.   [2] Gives each child an equal portion.

He allows his children maintenance according to their quality; otherwise it will make them base, acquaint them with bad company and sharking tricks.

In choosing a profession he is directed by his child's disposition : whose inclination is the strongest indenture to bind him to a trade, Yet he humours not his child when he makes an unworthy choice beneath himself, or rather for ease than use, pleasure than profit.

If his son prove wild, he doth not cast him off so far, but he marks the place where he lights. With the mother of Moses, he doth not suffer his son so to sink or swim, but he leaves one to stand afar off to watch what will become of him. He is careful, while he quencheth his luxury, not withal to put out his life.

He moves him to marriage rather by argument drawn for his good, than his own authority. It is a style too princely for a parent herein to will and command ; but sure he may will and desire. Affections like the conscience are rather to be led than drawn : and it is to be feared, they that marry where they do not love, will love where they do not marry.

He doth not give away his loaf to his children, and then come to them for a piece of bread. He holds the reins (though loosely) in his own hands, and keeps to reward duty and punish undutifulness ; yet on good occasion for his children's advancement he will depart from part of his means.   Base is their nature who will not ·have their branches lopped till their body be felled, and will let go none of their goods, as if it presaged their speedy death ; whereas it doth not follow that he that puts off his cloak must presently go to bed.

On his death-bed he bequeaths his blessing to all his children : nor rejoiceth he so much to leave them great portions, as honestly obtained.   Only money well and lawfully gotten is good and lawful money. And if he leaves his children young, he principally nominates God to be their guardian, and next Him is careful to appoint provident overseers.

THE GOOD CHILD.

He reverenceth the person of his parent, though old, poor, and froward. As his parent bare with him when a child, he bears with his parent if twice a child : nor doth his dignity above him cancel his duty unto him.   When Sir Thomas More was Lord Chancellor of England, and Sir John his father one of the judges of the King's Bench, he would in Westminster Hall beg his blessing of him on his knees.

He observes his lawful commands, and practiseth his precepts with all obedience. Having practised them himself, he entails his parent's precepts on his posterity. Therefore such instructions are by Solomon (Proverbs i. 9) compared to frontlets and chains (not to a suit of clothes, which serves but one, and quickly wears out, or out of fashion) which have in them real lasting worth, and are bequeathed as legacies to another age. The same counsels observed are chains to grace, which neglected, prove halters to strangle undutiful children.

He is patient under correction, and thankful after it. When Mr. West, formerly tutor (such I count in *loco parentis*) to Dr. Whitaker, was by him, then Regius Professor, created Doctor, Whitaker solemnly gave him thanks before the university for giving him correction when his young scholar.

In marriage he first and last consults with his father : when propounded, when concluded. He best bowls at the mark of his own contentment who, besides the aim of his own eye, is directed by his father, who is to give him the ground.

He is a stork to his parent, and feeds him in his old age. Not only if his father hath been a pelican, but though he hath been an ostrich unto him, and neglected him in his youth. He confines him not a long way off to a short pension, forfeited if he comes in his presence; but shews piety at home, and learns to requite his parent.

Such a child God commonly rewards with long life in this world. If he chance to die young, yet he lives long that lives well : and time mispent is not lived but lost. Besides, God is better than his promise, if he takes from him a long lease, and gives him a freehold of better value.

As for disobedient children. If preserved from the gallows they are reserved for the rack, to be tortured by their own posterity. One complained that never father had so undutiful a child as he had. Yes, said his son, with less grace than truth, my grandfather had.

I conclude this subject with the example of a pagan's son, which will shame most Christians. Pomponius Atticus, making the funeral oration at the death of his mother, did protest that, living with her threescore years and seven years, he was never reconciled unto her, *Se nunquam cum matre in gratium rediisse;* because (take the comment with the text) there never happened betwixt them the least jar which needed reconciliation.

THE GOOD MASTER.

He is the heart in the midst of his household, first up and last a-bed, if not in his person yet in his providence. In his carriage he aimeth at his own and his servant's good, and to advance both.

He oversees the works of his servants. One said *that the dust that fell from the master's shoes was the best compost to manure ground.* The lion out of state will not run whilst anyone looks upon him, but some servants out of slothfulness will not run except some do look upon them, spurred on with their master's eye. Chiefly he is careful exactly to take his servants' reckonings. If their master takes no account of them, they will make small account of him, and care not what they spend who are never brought to an audit.

The wages he contracts for he duly and truly pays. He never threatens his servant but rather presently corrects him.[1] Indeed conditional threatenings, with promise of pardon on amendment, are good and useful. Absolute threatenings torment more, reform less, making servants keep their faults

[1] Ephes. vi. 9.

and forsake their masters : wherefore herein he never passeth his word, but makes present payment, lest the creditor run away from the debtor.

In correcting his servant, he becomes not a slave to his own passion. If he perceives his servant incorrigible, so that he cannot wash the blackamoor, he washeth his hands of him, and fairly puts him away.

He is tender to his servant in his sickness and age, if crippled in his service his house is his hospital.

THE GOOD SERVANT.

He is one that out of conscience serves God in his master, and so hath the principle of obedience in himself. As for those servants who found their obedience on some external thing, with engines, they will go no longer than they are wound or weighed up.

He doth not dispute his master's lawful will, but doeth it. He loves to go about his business with cheerfulness. *God loveth a cheerful giver;* and Christ reproved the Pharisees for disfiguring their faces with a sad countenance. Fools! who to persuade men that angels lodged in their hearts, hung out a devil for a sign in their faces. Sure cheerfulness in doing renders a deed more acceptable ; not like those servants who doing their work unwillingly, their looks do enter a protestation against what their hands are doing.

He dispatcheth his business with quickness and ex-pedition. Hence the same English word speed signifies celerity and success ; the former in business of exe-cution causing the latter. Indeed haste and rashness are storms and tempests, breaking and wrecking busi-ness ; but nimbleness is a fair full wind, blowing it with speed to the haven. As he is good at hand, so he is good at length, continually and constantly careful in his service. Many servants, as if they had learned the nature of the besoms they use, are good for a few days, and afterwards grow unserviceable.

He disposeth not of his master's goods without his privity or consent : no not in the smallest matters. His answers to his master are true, direct, and dutiful. Just correction he bears patiently, and unjust he takes cheerfully.

THE GOOD WIDOW.

She is a woman whose head hath been quite cut off, and yet she liveth.

Her grief for her husband, though real, is moderate,

is no storm, but a still rain. Indeed some foolishly discharge the surplusage of their passions on themselves, tearing their hair, so that their friends, coming to the funeral, know not which most to bemoan, the dead husband, or the dying widow. Yet commonly it comes to pass that such widows' grief is quickly emptied.

Though going abroad sometimes about her business, she never makes it her business to go abroad. She is most careful of her credit, and tender of her modesty.

She loves to look on her husband's picture in the children he hath left her ; not foolishly fond over them for their father's sake (this were to kill them in honour of the dead), but giveth them careful education. Her husband's friends are ever her welcomest guests, whom she entertaineth with her best cheer, and with honourable mention of their friend's, and her husband's memory.

If she can speak little good of him, she speaks but little of him : so handsomely folding up her discourse, that his virtues are shewn outwards, and his vices wrapped up in silence. She is a champion for his credit if any speak against him.

She putteth her especial confidence in God's providence. Surely if he be *a father to the fatherless* it must needs follow that he is a husband to the widow.

And therefore she seeks to gain and keep his love unto her, by her constant prayer and religious life.

She will not mortgage her first husband's pawns, thereby to purchase the good-will of a second. If she marrieth (for which she has the apostle's decree, not to say mandate, *I will that the younger widows marry*), she will not abridge her children of that which justly belongs unto them. Surely a broken faith to the former is but a weak foundation to build thereon a loyal affection to a latter love. Yet if she becomes a mother-in-law, there is no difference betwixt her carriage to her own and her second husband's children, save that she is severest to her own, over whom she hath the sole jurisdiction. And if her second husband's children by a former wife commit a fault, she had rather bind them over to answer for it before their own father, than to correct them herself, to avoid all suspicion of hard using of them.

THE GOOD ADVOCATE.

He is one that will not plead that cause wherein his tongue must be confuted by his conscience. It is the praise of the Spanish soldier that, whilst all other nations are mercenary, and for money will serve on

any side, he will never fight against his own king ;
nor will our advocate against the sovereign truth,
plainly appearing to his conscience.

He not only hears but examines his client, and
pincheth the cause where he fears it is foundered.
For many clients in telling their case rather plead
than relate it, so that the advocate hears not the true
state of it, till opened by the adverse party. Surely
the lawyer who fills himself with instructions will
travel longest in the cause without tiring. Others
that are so quick in searching, seldom search to the
quick ; and those miraculous apprehensions who
understand more than all before the client hath told
half, run without their errand, and will return without
their answer.

If the matter be doubtful, he will only warrant his
own diligence. Yet some keep an assurance office in
their chamber, and will warrant any cause brought
unto them, as knowing that if they fail they lose
nothing but what long since was lost, their credit.

He makes not a Trojan siege of a suit, but seeks
to bring it to a set battle in a speedy trial. Yet
sometimes suits are continued by their difficulty the
potency and stomach of the parties, without any
default in the lawyer.

He is faithful to the side that first retains him.

Not like Demosthenes, who secretly wrote one oration for Phormio, and another in the same matter for Apolidorus his adversary.[1]

In pleading he shoots fairly at the head of the cause, and having fastened, no frowns nor favours shall make him let go his hold. Not snatching aside here and there to no purpose, speaking little in much, as it was said of Anaximenes, *That he had a flood of words, and a drop of reason.* His boldness riseth or falleth as he apprehends the goodness or badness of his cause.

He joys not to be retained in such a suit where all right in question is but a drop blown up with malice to be a bubble. Wherefore in such trivial matters he persuades his client to sound a retreat, and make a composition.

When his name is up his industry is not down, thinking to plead not by his study but his credit. Commonly physicians, like beer, are best when they are old, and lawyers, like bread, when they are young and new. But our advocate grows not lazy. And if a leading case be out of the road of his practice, he will take pains to trace it through his books, and prick the footsteps thereof wheresoever he finds it.

---

[1] Plutarch, in " Vita Demosth."

C

He is more careful to deserve than greedy to take fees. He accounts the very pleading of a poor widow's honest cause sufficient fees, as conceiving himself then the King of Heaven's advocate, bound *ex officio* to prosecute it.

We will respite him a while till he comes to be a judge.

THE GOOD PHYSICIAN.

Coming to his patient he persuades him to put his trust in God, the fountain of health. The neglect hereof hath caused the bad success of the best physicians : for God will manifest that though skill come mediately from him to be gotten by man's pains, success comes from him immediately to be disposed at his pleasure.

He hansels not his new experiments on the bodies of his patients ; letting loose mad recipes into the sick man's body, to try how well nature in him will fight against them, whilst himself stands by and sees the battle, except it be in desperate cases, when death must be expelled by death.

To poor people he prescribes cheap but wholesome medicines : not removing the consumption out of their bodies into their purses.

He brings not news with a false spy, that the coast is clear, till death surprises the sick man. I know physicians love to make the best of their patient's estate : first, it is improper that *Adjutores vitæ* should be *Nuncii mortis ;* secondly, none with their good-will will tell bad news ; thirdly, their fee may be the worse for it; fourthly, it is a confessing that their art is conquered ; fifthly, it will poison their patient's heart with grief, and make it break before the time. However, they may so order it, that the party may be informed of his dangerous condition, that he be not outed of this world before he be provided for another. When he can keep life no longer in, he makes a fair and easy passage for it to go out.

The Controversial Divine.

He is Truth's champion to defend her against all adversaries, atheists, heretics, schismatics, and erroneous persons whatsoever. His sufficiency appears in opposing, answering, moderating, and writing.

He engageth both his judgment and affections in opposing of falsehood. Not like country fencers, who play only to make sport, but like duellers indeed, as if for life and limb; chiefly if the question be of large prospect, and great concernings, he is zealous in the quarrel. Yet some, though their judgment weigh down on one side, the beam of their affections stand so even, they care not which part prevails.

In opposing a truth he dissembles himself her foe, to be her better friend. Wherefore he counts himself the greatest conqueror when truth hath taken him captive. With Joseph, having sufficiently sifted the matter in a disguise, he discovereth himself, *I am Joseph your brother*,[1] and then throws away his vizard. Dishonest they, who though the debt be satisfied, will never give up the bond, but continue wrangling when the objection is answered. He abstains from all foul and railing language. What! make the muses, yea, the graces scolds! He tyrannizeth not over a weak and undermatched adversary, but seeks rather to cover his weakness, if he be a modest man. In answering, he states the question and expounds the terms thereof. Otherwise, the disputants shall end where they ought to have begun, in differences about words, and be barbarians each to other, speaking in a language neither understand. If the question be of

[1] Gen. xiv. 4.

historical cognizance, he shews the pedigree thereof; who first brewed it, who first broached it, and sends the wandering error with a passport home to the place of its birth. In taking away an objection he not only puts by the thrust, but breaks the weapon. Some rather escape than defeat an argument; and though by such an evasion they may shut the mouth of the opponent, yet may they open the difficulty wider in the hearts of the hearers. But our answerer either fairly resolves the doubt, or else shows the falseness of the argument, by beggaring the opponent to maintain such a fruitful generation of absurdities as his argument hath begotten; or lastly, returns and retorts it back upon him again. The first way unties the knot; the second cuts it asunder; the third whips the opponent with the knot himself tied. Sure it is more honour to be a clear answerer than a cunning opposer because the latter takes advantage of man's ignorance, which is ten times more than his knowledge.

What his answers want in suddenness, they have in solidity. Indeed the speedy answer adds lustre to the disputation, and honour to the disputant; yet he makes good payment who, though he cannot presently throw the money out of his pocket, yet will pay it, if but going home to unlock his chest. Some there are not for speedy may be for sounder performance. When Melancthon, at the disputation of Ratisbon, was pressed with a shrewd argument by Ecchius, "I will answer thee," said he, "to-morrow." "Nay," said Ecchius, "do it now, or it's nothing worth." "Yea," said Melancthon, "I seek the truth, and not mine own credit, and therefore it will be as good if I answer thee to-morrow by God's assistance." In moderating, he sides with the answerer if the answerer sides with the truth. But, if he be conceited, and opinioned of his own sufficiency, he lets him swoon before he gives him any hot water. If a paradox-monger, loving to hold strange, yea, dangerous opinions, he counts it charity to suffer such a one to be beaten without mercy, that he may be weaned from his wilfulness. For the main he is so a staff to the answerer, that he makes him stand on his own legs.

He affects clearness and plainness in all his writings. Some men's heads are like the world before God said unto it, *Fiat lux.* These dark lanterns may shine to themselves, and understand their own conceits, but nobody else can have light from them. Some affect this darkness, that they may be accounted profound, whereas one is not bound to believe that all the water is deep that is muddy.

He is not curious in searching matters of no moment. Captain Martin Forbisher fetched from the farthest northern countries a ship's lading of mineral stones, as he thought, which afterwards were cast out to mend the highways.[1] Thus are they served, and miss their hopes, who long seeking, to extract hidden mysteries out of nice questions, leave them off, as useless at last. Antoninus Pius, for his desire to search to the least differences, was called *Cumini sector*, the carver of cummin seed. One need not be so accurate, for as soon shall one scour the spots out of the moon, as all ignorance out of man.

He neither multiplies needless, nor compounds necessary controversies. Sure they light on a labour in vain, who seek to make a bridge of reconciliation over the μέγα χάσμα betwixt papists and protestants; for though we go ninety-nine steps, they (I mean their church) will not come one to give us a meeting.

He is resolute and stable in fundamental points of religion. These are his fixed poles and axletree about which he moves, whilst they stand unmoveable. Some sail so long on the sea of controversies, tossed up and down, to and fro, *pro* and *con*, that the very ground to them seems to move, and their judgments

---

[1] Camden's "Elizab.," anno. 1576.

grow sceptical and unstable in the most settled points of divinity. When he cometh to preach, especially if to a plain auditory, with the Paracelsians he extracts an oil of the driest and hardest bodies, and knowing that knotty timber is unfit to build with, he edifies people with easy and profitable matter.

The True Church Antiquary.

He is a traveller into former times, whence he had learnt their language and fashions. If he meets with an old manuscript which hath the mark worn out of its mouth, and hath lost the date, yet he can tell the age thereof either by the phrase or character.

He baits at middle antiquity, but lodges not till he comes at that which is ancient indeed. Some scour off the rust of old inscriptions into their own souls, cankering themselves with superstition, having read so often *Orate pro anima,* that at last they fall a praying for the departed ; and they more lament the ruin of monasteries, than the decay and ruin of monks' lives, degenerating from their ancient piety and painfulness. Indeed a little skill in antiquity inclines a man to popery ; but depth in that study brings him about again to our religion. A nobleman who had heard of the extreme age of one dwelling not far off, made a journey to visit him, and finding an aged person sitting in the chimney corner, addressed himself unto him with admiration of his age, till his mistake was rectified ; for *Oh, Sir*, said the young old man, *I am not he whom you seek for, but his son; my father is further off in the field.* The same error is daily committed by the Romish Church, adorning the reverend brow and grey hairs of some ancient ceremonies, perchance but of some seven or eight hundred years' standing in the church, and mistake these for their fathers, of far greater age in the primitive times.

He desires to imitate the ancient fathers, as well in their piety as in their postures. Not only conforming his hands and knees, but chiefly his heart to their pattern. Oh the holiness of their living and painfulness of their preaching ! How full were they of mortified thoughts and heavenly meditations ! Let us not make the ceremonial part of their lives only canonical, and the moral part thereof altogether apocryphal ; imitating their devotion not in the fineness of the stuff, but only in the fashion of the making.

He carefully marks the declination of the church from the primitive purity. Observing how sometimes humble devotion was contented to lie down, whilst proud superstition got on her back. Yea, not only Frederick the emperor, but many a godly father some hundreds of years before, held the pope's stirrup, and by their well-meaning simplicity gave occasion to his future greatness. He takes notice how their rhetorical hyperboles were afterwards accounted the just measure of dogmatical truths: how plain people took them at their word in their funeral apostrophes to the dead; how praying for the departed brought the fuel, under which after ages kindled the fire of purgatory; how one ceremony begat another, there being no bounds in will-worship, wherewith one may sooner be wearied than satisfied; the inventors of new ceremonies endeavouring to supply in number what their conceits want in solidity; how men's souls being in the full speed and career of the historical use of pictures, could not stop short, but lash out into superstitions; how the fathers, veiling their bonnets to Rome in civil courtesy, when making honourable mention thereof, are interpreted by modern papists to have done it in adoration of the idol of the pope's infallibility. All these things he ponders in his heart, observing both the times and places when and where they happened.

He is not zealous for the introducing of old useless

ceremonies.   The mischief is, some that are most
violent to bring such in, are most negligent to preach
the cautions in using them ; and simple people, like
children in eating of fish, swallow bones and all, to
their danger of choking.   When many popish tricks
are abroad in the country, if then men meet with a
ceremony which is a stranger, especially if it can give
but a bad account of itself, no wonder if the watch
take it up for one on suspicion.

He is not peremptory but conjectural in doubtful
matters.   Not forcing others to his own opinion, but
leaving them to their own liberty ; not filling up all
with his own conjectures, to leave no room for other
men ; nor tramples he on their credits, if in them he
finds slips and mistakes.   For here our souls have but
one eye (the apostle saith, *we know in part*), be not
proud if that chance to come athwart thy seeing side,
which meets with the blind side of another.   He
thankfully acknowledgeth those by whom he hath
profited.   Base natured they, who when they have
quenched their own thirst, stop up, at least muddy, ·
the fountain.   But our antiquary, if he be not the
first founder of a commendable conceit, contents
himself to be a benefactor to it in clearing and
adorning it.

He doth not so adore the ancients as to despise the

moderns. Grant them but dwarfs, yet stand they on giants' shoulders, and may see the further. Sure, as stout champions of truth follow in the rear as ever marched in the front.

THE GENERAL ARTIST.

I know the general cavil against general learning is this, that he that sips of many arts, drinks of none. However, we must know that all learning, which is but one grand science, hath so homogeneal a body, that the parts thereof do with a mutual service relate to, and communicate strength and lustre each to other. Our artist, knowing language to be the key of learning, thus begins.

His tongue being but one by nature, he gets cloven by art and industry. Before the confusion of Babel all the world was one continent in language : since divided into several tongues, as several islands. Grammar is the ship, by benefit whereof we pass from one to another, in the learned languages generally spoken in no country. His mother-tongue was like the dull music of a monochord which by study he turns into the harmony of several instruments.

He first gaineth skill in the Latin and Greek

tongues. Hence he proceeds to the Hebrew, the
mother-tongue of the world. More pains than quickness of wit is required to get it, and with daily
exercise he continues it. As for the Arabic and
other oriental languages, he rather makes sallies
and incursions into them, than any solemn sitting
before them.

Then he applies his study to logic and ethics. The
latter makes a man's soul mannerly and wise; but as
for logic, that is the armoury of reason, furnished
with all offensive and defensive weapons. From
hence he raiseth his studies to the knowledge of
physics, the great hall of nature, and metaphysics,
the closet thereof; and is careful not to wade therein
so far, till by subtle distinguishing of notions he con-
founds himself.

He is skilful in rhetoric, which gives to speech
colour, as logic doth favour, and both together beauty.
Nor is he a stranger to poetry, which is music in
words ; nor to music which is poetry in sound : both
excellent sauce, but they have lived and died poor
that made them their meat.

Mathematics he moderately studieth to his great
contentment, using it as a ballast for his soul, yet to
fix it, not to stall it ; nor suffers he it to be so unmannerly as to jostle out other arts. Hence he makes

his progress into the study of history. Nestor, who lived three ages, was accounted the wisest man in the world. But the historian may make himself wise, by living as many ages as have passed since the beginning of the world. This directs him in his life, so that he makes the shipwrecks of others sea-marks to himself; yea accidents which others start from for their strangeness, he welcomes as his wonted acquaintance, having found precedents for them formerly. Without history a man's soul is purblind, seeing only the things which almost touch his eyes.

He is well seen in chronology, without which history is but a heap of tales. He is also acquainted with cosmography, treating of the world in whole joints; with chorography, shredding it into countries; and with topography, mincing it into particular places.

Thus taking these sciences in their general latitude, he hath finished the round circle or golden ring of the arts; only he keeps a place for the diamond to be set in, I mean for that predominant profession of law, physic, divinity or state policy, which he intends for his principal calling hereafter.

The Faithful Minister.

Conceive him now a graduate in arts, and entered into orders, according to the solemn form of the Church of England, and presented by some patron to a pastoral charge, or place equivalent, and then let us see how well he dischargeth his office.

He endeavours to get the general love and goodwill of his parish. This he doth not so much to make a benefit of them, as a benefit for them, that his ministry may be more effectual ; otherwise he may preach his own heart out before he preacheth anything into theirs. Yet he humours them not in his doctrine to get their love : he shall sooner get their good-will by walking uprightly, than by crouching and creeping. If pious living and painful labouring in his calling will not win their affections, he counts it gain to lose them. As for those who causelessly hate him, he pities and prays for them : and such there will be. I should suspect his preaching had no salt in it, if no galled horse did wince.

He is strict in ordering his conversation. It is said of one who preached very well, and lived very ill, *that when he was out of the pulpit, it was a pity he should ever go into it, and when he was in the pulpit, it was a pity he should ever come out of it :* but our minister lives sermons. And yet I deny not but dissolute men may by virtue of their office open heaven for others, and shut themselves out.

His behaviour towards his people is grave and courteous. Not too austere and retired ; which is laid to the charge of good Mr. Hooper the Martyr, that his rigidness frightened people from consulting with him. *Let your light,* saith Christ, *shine before men ;* whereas over-reservedness makes the brightest virtue burn dim. Especially he detesteth affected gravity, which is rather on men than in them, whereby some belie their register-book, antedate their age to seem far older than they are, and plait and set their brows in an affected sadness. Whereas St. Anthony the monk might have been known among hundreds of his order by his cheerful face, he having ever, though a most mortified man, a merry countenance.

He doth not clash God's ordinances together about precedency. Not making odious comparisons betwixt prayer and preaching, preaching and catechizing, public prayer and private, premeditate prayer and *extempore.* Our minister compounds all controversies betwixt God's ordinances, by praising them all, practising them all, and thanking God for them all. He counts the reading of common prayers to prepare him the better for preaching; and as one said if he did first toll the bell on one side, it made it afterwards ring out the better in his sermons.

He carefully catechiseth his people in the elements of religion. Even Luther did not scorn to profess himself a scholar of the catechism. By this catechising the gospel first got ground of popery, and let not our religion, now grown rich, be ashamed of that which first gave it credit and set it up, lest the Jesuits beat us at our own weapon. Through the want of this catechising, many who are well skilled in some dark out-corners of divinity have lost themselves in the beaten road thereof.

He will not offer to God of that which costs him nothing; but takes pains aforehand for his sermons. Demosthenes never made any oration on the sudden; yea, being called upon he never rose up to speak, except he had well studied the matter: and he was wont to say, *That he shewed how he honoured and reverenced the people of Athens, because he was careful what he spake unto them.* Indeed if our minister be surprised with a sudden occasion, he counts himself rather to be excused than commended, if, premeditating only the bones of his sermon, he clothes it with flesh *extempore.* As for those whose long custom

D

hath made preaching their nature, that they can discourse sermons without study, he accounts their examples rather to be admired than imitated.

Having brought his sermon into his head, he labours to bring it into his heart, before he preaches it to his people. Surely that preaching which comes from the soul most works on the soul.

He chiefly reproves the reigning sins of the time and place he lives in. We may observe that our Saviour never inveighed against idolatry, usury, sabbath-breaking amongst the Jews ; not that these were not sins, but they were not practised so much in that age, wherein wickedness was spun with a finer thread ; and therefore, Christ principally bent the drift of his preaching against spiritual pride, hypocrisy, and traditions then predominant amongst the people. Also our minister confuteth no old heresies which time hath confuted, nor troubles his auditory with such strange hideous cases of conscience, that it is more hard to find the case than the resolution. In public reproving of sin, he ever whips the vice and spares the person.

The places of Scripture he quotes are pregnant and pertinent. As for heaping up of many quotations, it smacks of a vain ostentation of memory. Besides, it is as impossible that the hearer should profitably retain them all, as that the preacher hath seriously perused them all ; yea, whilst the auditors stop their attention, and stoop down to gather an impertinent quotation, the sermon runs on, and they lose more substantial matter. His similes and illustrations are always familiar, never contemptible. Indeed reasons are the pillars of the fabric of a sermon, but similitudes are the windows which give the best lights. He avoids such stories whose mention may suggest bad thoughts to the auditors, and will not use a light comparison to make thereof a grave application for fear lest his poison go farther than his antidote.

He makes not that wearisome which should ever be welcome. Wherefore his sermons are of an ordinary length except on an extraordinary occasion.

He counts the success of his ministry the greatest preferment. Yet herein God hath humbled many painful pastors, in making them to be clouds to rain not over Arabia the Happy, but over the Stony or desert. Yet such pastors may comfort themselves that great is their reward with God in heaven, who measures it not by their success but endeavours. Besides, though they see not, their people may feel benefit by their ministry. Yea the preaching of the word in some places is like the planting of woods, where though no profit is received for twenty years together, it comes afterwards. And grant that God honours thee not to build his temple in thy parish, yet thou mayest with David provide metal and materials for Solomon thy successor to build it with.

To sick folk he comes sometimes before he is sent for, as counting his vocation a sufficient calling. None of his flock shall want the extreme unction of prayer and counsel. Against the communion especially he endeavours that Janus his temple be shut in the whole parish, and that all be made friends.

He is moderate in his tenets and opinions. Not that he gilds over lukewarmness in matters of moment with the title of discretion, but withal he is careful not to entitle violence in indifferent and unconcerning matters to be zeal. He is sociable, and willing to do any courtesy for his neighbour ministers. He willingly communicates his knowledge unto them. Surely the gifts and graces of Christians lay in common, till base envy made the first enclosure. He neither slighteth his inferiors, nor repineth at those who in parts and credit are above him. He loveth the company of his neighbour ministers. Sure as ambergris is nothing so sweet in itself as when it is compounded with other things, so both godly and learned men are gainers by communicating themselves to their neighbours.

He is careful in the discreet ordering of his own family. A good minister and a good father may well agree together. Our minister also is as hospitable as his estate will permit, and makes every alms two by his cheerful giving it. He loveth also to live in a well-repaired house, that he may serve God therein more cheerfully. A clergyman who built his house from the ground wrote in it this counsel to his successor,

"If thou dost find a house built to thy mind
Without thy cost,
Serve thou the more God and the poor ;
My labour is not lost."

Lying on his death-bed he bequeaths to each of his parishioners his precepts and example for a legacy: and they in requital erect every one a monument for him in their hearts. He is so far from that base jealousy that his memory should be outshined by a brighter successor, and from that wicked desire that his people may find his worth by the worthlessness of him that succeeds, that he doth heartily pray to God to provide them a better pastor after his decease. As for outward estate, he commonly lives in too bare pasture to die fat. It is well if he hath gathered any flesh, being more in blessing than bulk.

THE GOOD PARISHIONER.

We will only describe his church reference; his civil part hath and shall be met with under other heads.   Conceive him to live under such a faithful minister as before was charactered, as, either judging charitably that all pastors are such, or wishing heartily that they were.   ·

Though near to the church he is not far from God. Otherwise if his distance from the church be great, his diligence is the greater to come thither in season. He is timely at the beginning of common prayer. Some negligent persons never hear prayers begun or sermon ended: the confession being passed before they come, and the blessing not come before they are passed away.

In sermons he sets himself to hear God in the minister.   Therefore divesting himself of all prejudice he hearkens very attentively; it is a shame when the church itself is cœmeterium, wherein the living sleep above ground as the dead do beneath.

At every point that concerns himself, he turns down a leaf in his heart, and rejoiceth that God's word hath pierced him, as hoping that whilst his soul smarts it heals.   And as it is no manners for him that hath good venison before him to ask whence it came, but rather fairly to fall to it, so hearing an excellent sermon, he never enquires whence the preacher had it, or whether it 'was not before in print, but falls aboard to practise it.

He accuseth not his minister of spite for particularizing him.   It does not follow that the archer aimed because the arrow hit.   Rather our parishioner reasoneth thus : if my sin be notorious, how could the minister miss it ; if secret, how could he hit it without God's direction? ' One causelessly disaffected to his minister, complained that he in his last sermon had personally inveighed against him, and accused him thereof to a grave religious gentleman in the parish. *Truly*, said the gentleman, *I had thought in his sermon he had meant me, for it touched my heart.*   This rebated the edge of the other's anger.

His tithes he pays willingly with cheerfulness. How many part with God's portions grudgingly, or else pinch it in the paying ! *Decimum*, the tenth, amongst the Romans was ever taken for what was best or biggest.   It falls out otherwise in paying of tithes, where the least and leanest are shifted off to make that number.

He hides not himself from any parish-office which

seek for him. If chosen churchwarden he is not busily idle, rather to trouble than reform; presenting all things but those which he should. If overseer of the poor, he is careful the rates be made indifferent (whose inequality oftentimes is more burdensome than the sum) and well disposed of. He measures not people's wants by their clamorous complaining, and dispenseth more to those that deserve than to them that only need relief.

He is bountiful in contributing to the repair of God's house. For though he be not of their opinion who would have the churches under the gospel conformed to the magnificence of Solomon's temple, whose porch would serve us for a church, and adorn them so gaudily, that devotion is more distracted than raised, and men's souls rather dazzled than lightened; yet he conceives it fitting that such sacred places should be handsomely and decently maintained.

He is respectful to his minister's widow and posterity for his sake. My prayer shall be, that ministers' widows and children may never stand in need of such relief, and may never want such relief when they stand in need.

THE GOOD LANDLORD.

Is one that lets his land on a reasonable rate, so that the tenant, by employing his stock and using his industry, may make an honest livelihood thereby, to maintain himself and his children.

His rent doth quicken his tenant, but not gall him. Indeed it is observed that where landlords are very easy, the tenants, out of their own laziness seldom thrive, contenting themselves to make up the just measure of their rent, and not labouring for any surplusage of estate. But our landlord puts some metal into his tenant's industry, yet not granting him too much, lest the tenant revenge the landlord's cruelty to him upon his land.

Yet he raiseth his rents, or fines, equivalent, in some proportion to the present price of other commodities. If, therefore, our landlord should let his rents stand still as his grandfather left them, whilst other wares daily go on in price, he must needs be cast far behind in his estate.

What he sells or sets to his tenant, he suffers him quietly to enjoy according to his covenants. This is a great joy to a tenant, though he buys dear to possess without disturbance.

He rejoiceth to see his tenants thrive. Yea he counts it a great honour to himself when he perceiveth that God blesseth their endeavours, and that they come forward in the world. I close up with this pleasant story. A farmer rented a grange generally reported to be haunted by fairies, and paid a shrewd rent for the same at each half year's end. Now a gentleman asked him how he durst be so hardy as to live in the house, and whether no spirits did trouble him. *Truth*, said the farmer, *there be two saints in heaven vex me more than all the devils in hell, namely the Virgin Mary and Michael the archangel;* on whose days he paid his rent.

THE GOOD SCHOOLMASTER.

There is scarce any profession in the commonwealth more necessary which is so slightly performed. The reasons whereof I conceive to be these: First, young scholars make this calling their refuge, yea, perchance, before they have taken any degree in the university, commence schoolmasters in the country, as if nothing else were required to set up this profession but only a rod and a ferula. Secondly, others who are able, use it only as a passage to better preferment, to patch the rents in their present fortune, till they can provide a new one, and betake themselves to some more gainful calling.   Thirdly, they are disheartened from doing their best with the miserable reward which in some places they receive, being masters to the children, and slaves to their parents. Fourthly, being grown rich, they grow negligent, and scorn to touch the school but by the proxy of an usher.   But see how well our schoolmaster behaves himself.

His genius inclines him with delight in his profession.   Some men had as lief be schoolboys as schoolmasters, to be tied to the school as Cooper's Dictionary and Scapula's Lexicon are chained to the desk therein, and though great scholars, and skilful in other arts, are bunglers in this: but God of his goodness hath fitted several men for several callings, that the necessity of church and state, in all conditions, may be provided for.   So that he who beholds the fabric thereof may say, God hewed out this stone, and appointed it to lie in this very place ; for it would fit none other so well, and here it doth most excellent. And thus God mouldeth some for a schoolmaster's life, undertaking it with desire and delight, and discharging it with dexterity and happy success.

He studies his scholars' natures as carefully as they

their books ; and ranks their dispositions into several forms. And though it may seem difficult for him in a great school to descend to all particulars, yet experienced schoolmasters may quickly make a grammar of boys' natures, and reduce them all, saving some few exceptions, to these general rules.

1. Those that are ingenious and industrious. The conjunction of two such planets in a youth presage much good unto him. To such a lad a frown may be a whipping, and a whipping a death ; yea, where their master whips them once, shame whips them all the week after. Such natures he useth with all gentleness.

2. Those that are ingenious and idle. These think with the hare in the fable, that running with snails (so they count the rest of their schoolfellows), they shall come soon enough to the post, though sleeping a good while before their starting. Oh, a good rod would finely take them napping !

3. Those that are dull and diligent. Wines the stronger they be the more lees they have when they are new. Many boys are muddy-headed till they be clarified with age, and such afterwards prove the best. Bristol diamonds are both bright, and squared and pointed by nature, and yet are soft and worthless; whereas Orient ones in India are rough and rugged

naturally. Hard, rugged, and dull natures of youth acquit themselves afterwards the jewels of the country, and therefore their dulness at first is to be borne with, if they be diligent. That schoolmaster deserves to be beaten himself, who beats nature in a boy for a fault. And I question whether all the whipping in the world can make their parts, who are naturally sluggish, rise one minute before the hour nature hath appointed.

4. Those that are invincibly dull and negligent also. Correction may reform the latter, not amend the former. All the whetting in the world can never set a razor's edge on that which hath no steel in it. Such boys he consigneth over to other professions. Shipwrights and bootmakers will choose those crooked pieces of timber which other carpenters refuse. Those may make excellent merchants and mechanics who will not serve for scholars.

He is able, diligent, and methodical in his teaching ; not leading them rather in a circle than forwards. He minces his precepts for children to swallow, hanging clogs on the nimbleness of his own soul, that his scholars may go along with him.

He is, and will be known to be an absolute monarch in his school. If he hath a stubborn youth, correction-proof, he debaseth not his authority by contesting

with him, but fairly, if he can, puts him away before
his obstinacy hath infected others.

THE GOOD MERCHANT.

Is one who by his trading claspeth the islands to
the continent, and one country to another. An excellent gardener, who makes England bear wine, and
oil, and spices ; he wrongs neither himself nor the
commonwealth, nor private chapmen who buy commodities of him. As for his behaviour towards the
commonwealth, it far surpasses my skill to give any
rules thereof; only this I know, that to export things
of necessity and to bring in foreign needless toys
makes a rich merchant and a poor kingdom.

He wrongs not the buyer in number, weight, or
measure. These are the landmarks of all trading,
which must not be removed : for such cozenage were
worse than open felony. First, because they rob a
man of his purse, and never bid him stand. Secondly,
because highway thieves defy, but these pretend
justice. Thirdly, as much as lies in their power, they
endeavour to make God accessory to their cozenage,
deceiving by pretending his weights. For God is the

principal clerk of the market. *All the weights of the bag are his work.*[1]

He never warrants any ware for good, but what is so indeed. Otherwise he is a thief, and may be a murderer, if selling such things as are applied inwardly. Besides in such a case he counts himself guilty if he selleth such wares as are bad, though without his knowledge, if avouching them for good ; because he may, professeth, and is bound to be master in his own mystery, and therefore in conscience must recompense the buyer's loss except he gives him an item to buy it at his own adventure.

He either tells the faults in his ware, or abates proportionably in the price he demands : for then the low value shows the viciousness of it. Yet commonly when merchants depart with their commodities, we hear, as in funeral orations, all the virtues, but none of the faults thereof.

He never demands out of distance of the price he intends to take : if not always within the touch, yet within the reach of what he means to sell for. Now, we must know there be four several prices of vendible things. First, the price of the market which ebbs and flows according to the plenty or scarcity of coin,

[1] Prov. xvi. II.

commodities, and chapmen. Secondly, the price of friendship, which perchance is more giving than selling, and therefore not so proper at this time. Thirdly, the price of fancy, as twenty pounds or more for a dog or hawk, when no such inherent worth can naturally be in them, but by the buyer's and seller's fancy reflecting on them. Yet I believe the money may be lawfully taken : First, because the seller sometimes on those terms is as loth to forego it, as the buyer is willing to have it ; and I know no standard herein whereby men's affections may be measured. Secondly, it being a matter of pleasure, and men able and willing, let them pay for it. Lastly, there is the price of cozenage, which our merchant from his heart detests and abhors.

He makes not advantage of his chapman's ignorance, chiefly if referring himself to his honesty : where the seller's conscience is all the buyer's skill, who makes him both seller and judge, so that he doth not so much ask as order what he must pay. When one told old Bishop Latimer that the cutler had cozened him, in making him pay twopence for a knife, not in those days worth a penny ; *No*, quoth Latimer, *he cozened not me, but his own conscience.* On the other side, St. Augustine tells us of a seller, who out of ignorance asked for a book far less than it was worth; and the buyer (conceive himself to be the man if you please) of his own accord gave him the full value thereof.

He makes not the buyer pay the shot for his prodigality; as when the merchant, through his own ignorance or ill husbandry, hath bought dear, he will not bring in his unnecessary expenses on the buyer's score; and in such a case he is bound to sell cheaper than he bought.

Selling by retail, he may justify the taking of greater gain, because of his care, pains, and cost of fetching those ware from the fountain, and in parcelling and dividing them. Yea, because retailers trade commonly with those who have least skill what they buy, and commonly sell to the poorer sort of people, they must be careful not to grate on their necessity.

But how long shall I be retailing our rules to this merchant? it would employ a casuist an apprenticeship of years: take our Saviour's wholesale rule: *Whatsoever ye would have men do unto you, do you unto them, for this is the law and the prophets.*

The Good Yeoman.

Is a gentleman in ore, whom the next age may see refined, and is the wax capable of a gentle impression, when the prince shall stamp it. Wise Solon, who accounted Tellus the Athenian the most happy man for living privately on his own lands, would surely have pronounced the English yeomanry a fortunate condition, living in the temperate zone, betwixt greatness and want, an estate of people almost peculiar to England. France and Italy are like a die, which hath no points between sink and ace, nobility and peasantry. Their walls, though high, must needs be hollow, wanting filling stones. Indeed Germany hath her boors, like our yeomen, but by a tyrannical appropriation of nobility to some few ancient famiiies, their yeomen are excluded from ever rising higher to clarify their bloods. In England, the temple of honour is bolted against none who have passed through the temple of virtue ; nor is a capacity to be gentle denied to our yeoman, who thus behaves himself.

He wears russet clothes, but makes golden payment, having tin in his buttons, and silver in his pocket. If he chance to appear in clothes above his rank, it is to grace some great man with his service, and then he blusheth at his own bravery. Otherwise he is the surest landmark, whence foreigners may take aim of the ancient English customs, the gentry more floating after foreign fashions.

In his house he is bountiful both to strangers and poor people. Some hold when hospitality died in England, she gave her last groan amongst the yeomen of Kent. And still at our yeoman's table you shall have as many joints as dishes: no meat disguised with strange sauces; no straggling joint of a sheep in the midst of a pasture of grass, beset with salads on every side, but solid substantial food. Here you have that which in itself is good made better by the store of it, and best by the welcome to it.

He improveth his land to a double value by his good husbandry. Some grounds that wept with water, or frowned with thorns, by draining the one, and clearing the other, he makes both to laugh and sing with corn. By marl and limestones burnt, he bettereth his ground, and his industry worketh miracles, by turning stones into bread. Conquest and good husbandry both enlarge the king's dominions: the one by the sword, making the acres

more in number ; the other by the plough, making
the same acres more in value.

The neighbour gentry court him for his acquaintance, which either he modestly waiveth, or thankfully
accepteth, but no way greedily desireth. He insults
not on the ruins of a decayed gentleman, but pities
and relieves him, and as he is called Goodman, he
desires to answer to the name, and to be so indeed.

THE HANDICRAFTSMAN.

He is a necessary member in a commonwealth.
His trade is such whereby he provides things necessary for mankind, or else his trade contributeth to
man's lawful pleasure. God is not so hard a master
but that he alloweth his servants sauce, besides
hunger, to eat with their meat.

The wares he makes show good to the eye, but
prove better to the use. For he knows if he sets his
mark, the tower-stamp of his credit, on any bad
wares, he sets a deeper brand on his own conscience.

By his ingeniousness he leaves his art better than
he found it. Herein the Hollanders are excellent,
where children get their living, when but newly they
have gotten their life, by their industry. Indeed

nature may seem to have made those Netherlanders the younger brethren of mankind, allowing them little land, and that also standing in daily fear of a double deluge of the sea and the Spaniard : but such is their painfulness and ingenuity, hating laziness as much as they love liberty, that what commodities grow not on their country by nature, they graft on it by art, and have wonderfully improved all making of manufactures, stuffs, clocks, watches.

He is willing to communicate his skill to posterity. An invention, though found, is lost if not imparted.

He seldom attaineth to any great estate : except his trade hath some outlets and excursions into whole-sale and merchandise; otherwise, mere artificers cannot heap up much wealth. It is difficult for gleaners without stealing whole sheaves to fill a barn. His chief wealth consisteth in enough, and that he can live comfortably, and leave his children the in-heritance of their education. I should now come to give description of the day labourer (of whom we have only a dearth in a plentiful harvest), but seeing his character is so coincident with the hired servant, it may well be spared. And now we will rise from the hand to the arm, and come to describe the soldier.

THE GOOD SOLDIER.

A soldier is one of a lawful, necessary, commendable, and honourable profession. Now, though many hate soldiers as the twigs of the rod war, wherewith God scourgeth wanton countries into repentance, yet is their calling so needful, that were not some soldiers, we must all be soldiers, daily employed to defend our own.

He keepeth a clear and quiet conscience in his breast, which otherwise will gnaw out the roots of all valour; for vicious soldiers are compassed with enemies on all sides. None fitter to go to war than those who have made their peace with God in Christ; for such a man's soul is an impregnable fort; it cannot be scaled with ladders, for it reacheth up to heaven; nor can it be broken by batteries, for it is walled with brass; nor undermined by pioneers, for he is founded on rock; nor betrayed by treason, for faith itself keeps it; nor be burnt by grenades, for he can quench the fiery darts of the devil; nor be forced by famine, for *a good conscience is a continual feast.* He chiefly avoids those sins to which soldiers are taxed as most subject.

He counts his prince's lawful command to be his sufficient warrant to fight. In a defensive war, when his country is hostilely invaded, it is a pity but his neck should hang in suspense with his conscience that doubts to fight; in offensive war, though the case be harder, the common soldier is not to dispute, but do his prince's command. Otherwise princes, before they levy an army of soldiers, must first levy an army of casuists and confessors, to satisfy each scrupulous soldier in point of right to the war, and the most cowardly will be the most conscientious to multiply doubts eternally. Besides causes of war are so complicated and perplexed, so many things falling in the prosecution, as may alter the original state thereof, and private soldiers have neither calling nor ability to dive into such mysteries. But if the conscience of a councillor or commander-in-chief remonstrates in himself the unlawfulness of this war, he is bound humbly to represent to his prince his reasons against it.

He esteemeth all hardship easy through hopes of victory. Moneys are the sinews of war, yet if these sinews should chance to be shrunk, and pay casually fall short, he takes a fit of this convulsion patiently; he is contented though in cold weather his hands must be their own fire, and warm themselves with working; though he be better armed against their enemies than the weather, and his corselet wholler than his clothes; though he hath more fasts and vigils in his almanack than the Romish church did ever enjoin; he patiently endureth drought for desire of honour, and one thirst quencheth another.

He looks at and also through his wages at God's glory, and his country's good. He counts his pay an honourable addition, but no valuable compensation for his pains.

He attends with all readiness on the commands of the general: rendering up his own judgment in obedience to the will and pleasure of his leader, and by an implicit faith believing all is best which he enjoineth; lest otherwise he be served as the French soldier was in Scotland some eighty years since, who first mounted the bulwark of a fort besieged, whereupon ensued the gaining of the fort: but Mareschal de Thermes, the French general, first knighted him and then hanged him within an hour after, because he had done it without commandment.[1]

He will not in a bravery expose himself to needless peril. It is madness to halloo in the ears of sleeping temptation, to awaken it against one's self, or to go

---

[1] Hollman, in his book of "The Ambassador."

out of his calling to find a danger; but if a danger meets him as he walks in his vocation, he neither stands still, starts aside, nor steps backward, but either goes over it with valour, or under it with patience.

But when God and his prince calls for him our soldier had rather die ten times than once survive his credit. Though life be sweet, it shall not flatter the palate of his soul, as with the sweetness of life to make him swallow down the bitterness of an eternal disgrace. He begrudgeth not to get to his side the probability of victory by the certainty of his own death, and flieth from nothing so much as from the mention of flying. And though some say he is a madman that will purchase honour so dearly with his blood, as that he cannot live to enjoy what he hath bought, our soldier knows that he shall possess the reward of his valour with God in heaven, and also, making the world his executor, leave to it the rich inheritance of his memory.

Yet in some cases he counts it no disgrace to yield, where it is impossible to conquer; as when swarms of enemies crowd about him, so that he shall rather be stifled than wounded to death : in such case if quarter be offered him, he may take it with more honour than the other can give it ; and if he throws up his desperate game, he may happily win the next, whereas if he play it out to the last, he shall certainly lose it and himself. But if he fall into the hand of a barbarous enemy, whose giving quarter is but reprieving him for a more ignominious death, he had rather disburse his life at the present, than to take day to fall into the hands of such remorseless creditors.

He makes none the object of his cruelty, who cannot be the object of his fear. He counts it murder to kill any in cold blood, especially when soldiers have suffered long in a hard siege, it is pardonable what present passion doth with a sudden thrust; but a premeditated back-blow in cold blood is base.

He doth not barbarously abuse the bodies of his dead enemies. We find that Hercules was the first (the most valiant are ever the most merciful) that ever suffered his enemies to carry away their dead bodies after they have been put to the sword. Belike before the time they cruelly cut the corpses in pieces, or cast them to the wild beasts.

He is willing and joyful to embrace peace on good conditions. He is quiet and painful in peace as courageous in war, but we leave our soldier, seeking by his virtues to ascend from a private place, by the degrees of sergeant, lieutenant, captain, colonel, till he come to be a general, and then in the next book, God willing, you shall have his example.

THE GOOD SEA CAPTAIN.

His military part is concurrent with that of the soldier already described : he differs only in some sea properties, which we will now set down.   Conceive him now in a man-of-war, with his letters of mart, well armed, victualled, and appointed, and see how he acquits himself.   The more power he hath, the more careful he is not to abuse it.   Indeed, a sea captain is a king in the island of a ship.

He is careful in observing of the Lord's day.   He hath a watch in his heart, though no bells in a steeple to proclaim that day by ringing to prayers.

He is as pious and thankful when a tempest is past, as devout when it is present : not clamorous to receive mercies, and tongue-tied to return thanks.   Many mariners are calm in a storm, and storm in a calm, blustering with oaths.   In a tempest, it comes to their turn to be religious whose piety is but a fit of the wind, and when it is allayed, their devotion is ended.

Escaping many dangers makes him not presumptuous to run into them.

He counts it a disgrace, seeing all mankind is one family, sundry countries but several rooms, that we who dwell in the parlour (so he counts Europe) should not know the out-lodgings of the same house, and the world be scarce acquainted with itself before it be dissolved from itself at the day of judgment.

He daily sees and duly considers God's wonders in the deep. Tell me, ye naturalists, who sounded the first march and retreat to the tide, *Hither shalt thou come, and no further?* Why doth not the water recover his right over the earth, being higher in nature? Whence came the salt, and who first boiled it, which made so much brine? When the winds are not only wild in a storm, but even stark mad in a hurricane, who is it that restores them again to their wits, and brings them asleep in a calm? Who made the mighty whales, who swim in a sea of water, and have a sea of oil swimming in them? Who first taught the water to imitate the creatures on land, so that the sea is the stable of horse-fishes, the stall of kine-fishes, the stye of hog-fishes, the kennel of dog-fishes, and in all things the sea the ape of the land? Whence grows the ambergris in the sea, which is not so hard to find where it is, as to know what it is? Was not God the first shipwright, and all vessels on the water descended from the loins, or the ribs rather, of Noah's ark ?   Or else who durst be so bold, with a few crooked boards nailed together, a stick standing upright, and a rag tied to it, to adventure into the ocean ?   What load-stone first touched the loadstone ; or how first fell it in love with the north, rather affecting that cold climate than the pleasant east, or fruitful south or west ? how comes that stone to know more than men, and find the way to the land in a mist ?   In most of these men take sanctuary at *occulta qualitas*, and complain that the room is dark when their eyes are blind. Indeed they are God's wonders, and that seaman the greatest wonder of all for his blockishness, who, seeing them daily, neither takes notice of them, admires at them, nor is thankful for them.

THE TRUE GENTLEMAN.

We will consider him in his birth, breeding, and behaviour.

He is extracted from ancient and worshipful parentage, his blood must needs be well purified who is gently born on both sides.

If his birth be not, at least his qualities are generous.

What if he cannot with the Hevenninghams of Suffolk count five and twenty knights of his family,[1] or tell sixteen knights successively with the Tilneys of Norfolk,[2] or with the Nauntons show where their ancestors had seven hundred pounds a year before or at the Conquest.[3] Yet he hath endeavoured by his own deserts to ennoble himself. Thus valour makes him son to Cæsar; learning entitles him kinsman to Tully; and piety reports him nephew to godly Constantine. It graceth a gentleman of low descent and high desert, when he will own the meanness of his parentage. How ridiculous it is when men brag that their families are more ancient than the moon, which all know are later than the star which some seventy years since shined in Cassiopeia!

He is not in his youth possessed with the great hopes of his possession. No flatterer reads constantly in his ears a survey of the lands he is to inherit. This hath made many boys' thoughts swell so great, that they could never be kept in compass afterwards. Only his parents acquaint him that he is the next undoubted heir to correction, if misbehaving himself; and he finds no more favour from his schoolmaster than his schoolmaster finds diligence in him,

[1] Weaver's "Fun. Mon.," p. 854.
[2] *Idem.* p. 818.   [3] *Idem.* p. 758.

whose rod respects persons no more than bullets are partial in a battle.

At the university he is so studious as if he intended learning for his profession. He knows well that cunning is no burthen to carry, as paying neither porterage by land, nor poundage by sea. Yea, though to have land be a good first, yet to have learning is the surest second, which may stand to it when the other may chance to be taken away.

As for the hospitality, the apparel, the travelling, the company, the recreations, the marriage of gentlemen, they are described in several of the following chapters. A word or two of his behaviour in the country.

He is courteous and affable to his neighbours. As the sword of the best tempered metal is most flexible, so the truly generous are most pliant and courteous in their behaviour to their inferiors.

He delights to see himself and his servants well mounted: therefore he loveth good horsemanship. He furnisheth and prepareth himself in peace against time of war; lest it is too late to learn when his skill is to be used. He approves himself courageous when brought to the trial, as well remembering the custom which is used at the creation of knights of the bath, wherein the king's master cook cometh forth, and presenteth his great knife to the new-made knights, admonishing them to be faithful and valiant, otherwise he threatens them that that very knife is prepared to cut off their spurs.[1]

If the commission of the peace finds him out, he faithfully discharges it. I say, finds him out, for a public office is a guest which receives the best usage from them who never invited it. And though he declined the place, the country knew to prize his worth, who would be ignorant of his own. He compounds many petty differences betwixt his neighbours, which are easier ended in his own porch than in Westminster Hall; for many people think, if once they have fetched a warrant from a justice, they have given earnest to follow the suit, though otherwise the matter be so mean that the next night's sleep would have bound both parties to the peace, and made them as good friends as ever before.

Yet, he connives not at the smothering of punishable faults. He hates that practice, as common as dangerous amongst country people, who, having received again the goods which were stolen from them, partly out of foolish pity, and partly out of covetousness to save charges in prosecuting the law,

---

[1] Mr. Selden in his "Titles of Honour," p. 820.

let the thief escape unpunished. Thus whilst private losses are repaired, the wounds to the commonwealth, in the breach of the laws, are left uncured ; and thus the petty larceners are encouraged into felons, and afterwards are hanged for pounds, because never whipped for pence, who, if they had felt the cord, had never been brought to the halter.

If chosen a member of parliament, he is willing to do his country service. If he be no rhetorician to raise affections (yea, Mercury was a greater speaker than Jupiter himself), he counts it great wisdom to be the good manager of yea and nay. The slow pace of his judgment is recompensed by the swift following of his affections, when his judgment is once soundly informed. And here we leave him in consultation, wishing him, with the rest of his honourable society, all happy success.

Of Hospitality.

Hospitality is threefold ; for one's family, this is of necessity : for strangers, this is courtesy : for the poor, this is charity. To keep a disorderly house is the way to keep neither house nor lands. For whilst they keep the greatest roaring, their state steals away in the greatest silence.

Measure not thy entertainment of a guest by his estate but thine own. Because he is a lord, forget not that thou art but a gentleman.

Mean men's palates are best pleased with fare rather plentiful than various, solid than dainty. Dainties will cost more and content less, to those who are not critical enough to distinguish them.

Occasional entertainment of men greater than thyself is better than solemn inviting them. Then short warning is thy large excuse : whereas, if thou dost not overdo thy estate, thou shalt underdo his expectation, for thy feast will be but his ordinary fare.

Those are ripe for charity who are withered with age or impotency. Especially if maimed in following their calling; add to these, those that with diligence fight against poverty, though neither conquer till death make it a drawn battle. Expect not, but prevent, their craving of thee : for God forbid the heavens should never rain till the earth first opens her mouth seeing some grounds will sooner burn than chap!

The house of correction is the fittest hospital for those cripples whose legs are lame through their own laziness. Surely King Edward the Sixth was as truly charitable in granting bridewell for the punishment of sturdy rogues, as in giving St. Thomas's Hospital for the relief of the poor. I have done with this subject, only I desire rich men to awaken hospitality, which one saith, since the year 1572 hath in a manner been laid asleep in the grave of Edward Earl of Derby.

OF JESTING.

Harmless mirth is the best cordial against the consumption of the spirits ; wherefore jesting is not unlawful if it trespasseth not in quantity, quality, or season.

It is good to make a jest, but not to make a trade of jesting. The Earl of Leicester knowing that Queen Elizabeth was much delighted to see a gentleman dance well, brought the master of a dancing school to dance before her. *Pish*, said the queen, *it is his profession, I will not see him.* She liked it not where it was a master quality, but where it attended on other perfections. The same may we say of jesting. Jest not with the two-edged sword of God's word.[1] Will nothing please thee to wash thy hands in, but the font, or to drink healths in, but the church

[1] Heb. iv. 12.

chalice? And know the whole art is learnt at the first admission, and profane jests will come without calling. Wherefore, if without thine intention, and against thy will, by chance-medley thou hittest Scripture in ordinary discourse, yet fly to the city of refuge, and pray to God to forgive thee.

Wanton jests make fools laugh, and wise men frown. Seeing we are civilized Englishmen, let us not be naked savages in our talk. Let not thy jests, like mummy, be made of dead men's flesh. Abuse not any that are departed; for to wrong their memories is to rob their ghosts of their winding-sheets.

Scoff not at the natural defects of any which are not in their power to amend. Oh, it is cruelty to beat a cripple with his own crutches! Neither flout any for his profession, if honest, though poor and painful. Mock not a cobbler for his black thumbs.

He that relates another man's wicked jests with delight, adopts them to be his own. Purge them therefore from their poison. If the profaneness may be severed from the wit, it is like a lamprey; take out the sting in the back, it may make good meat. But if the staple conceit consists in profaneness, then it is a viper, all poison, and meddle not with it. He that will lose his friend for a jest, deserves to die a beggar by the bargain. Yet some think their conceits, like mustard, not good except they bite. We read that all those who were born in England the year after the beginning of the great mortality, 1349,[1] wanted their four cheek-teeth. Such let thy jests be, that they may not grind the credit of thy friend, and make not jests so long till thou becomest one. No time to break jests when the heart-strings are about to be broken. No more showing of wit when the head is to be cut off, like the dying man, who when the priest coming to him to give him extreme unction, asked of him where his feet were, answered, *at the end of my legs*. But at such a time jests are an unmannerly *crepitus ingenii*, and let those take heed who end here with Democritus, that they begin not with Heraclitus.

On Self Praising.

He whose own worth doth speak, need not speak his own worth. Such boasting sounds proceed from emptiness of desert : whereas the conquerors in the Olympian games did not put on the laurels on their own heads, but waited till some other did it.

It showeth more wit but no less vanity to commend

---

[1] Tho. Walsingham, in eodem anno.

one's self not in a straight line, but by reflection. Some sail to the port of their own praise by a side wind; as when they dispraise themselves; or when they flatter another to his face, tossing the ball to him that he may throw it back again to them; or when they commend that quality wherein themselves excel, in another man, though absent, whom all know far their inferior in that faculty.

Self praising comes most naturally from a man when it comes most violently from him in self defence. For though modesty binds a man's tongue to the peace in this point, yet being assaulted in his credit he may stand upon his guard, and then he doth not so much praise as purge himself. One braved a gentleman to his face, that in skill and valour he came far behind him : *It is true*, said the other, *for when I fought with you, you ran away before me.* In such a case, it was well returned, and without any just aspersion of pride.

OF TRAVELLING.

It is a good accomplishment to a man if first the stock be well grown whereon travel is grafted, and these rules observed before, in, and after his going abroad.

Travel not early before thy judgment be risen ; lest thou observest rather shows than substance, marking alone pageants, pictures, beautiful buildings, etc.

Get the language, in part, without which key thou shalt unlock little of moment. It is a great advantage to be one's own interpreter. Object not that the French tongue learnt in England must be unlearnt again in France ; for it is easier to add than begin, and to pronounce than to speak. Be well settled in thine own religion, lest travelling out of England into Spain, thou goest out of God's blessing into the warm sun. But if first thou be well grounded, fooleries shall rivet thy faith the faster, and travel shall give thee confirmation in that baptism thou didst receive at home.

Know most of the rooms of thy native country before thou goest over the threshold thereof. Especially seeing England presents thee with so many observables. But late writers lack nothing but age, and home-wonders but distance, to make them admired.

Be wise in choosing objects, diligent in marking, careful in remembering of them ; yet herein men much follow their own humours. One asked a barber, who never before had been at the court, what he saw there ? *Oh*, said he, *the king was excellently well trimmed!* Thus merchants most mark foreign havens, exchanges, and marts; soldiers note forts, armouries, and magazines; scholars listen after libraries, disputations, and professors; statesmen observe courts of justice, councils, etc. Everyone is partial to his own profession.

Labour to distil and unite unto thyself the scattered perfections of several nations. But, as it was said of one who with more industry than judgment frequented a college library, and commonly made use of the worst notes he met with in any authors, that he *weeded* the library, many weed foreign countries. Others bring home just nothing; and because they singled not themselves from their countrymen, though some years beyond sea, were never out of England.

Let discourse rather be easily drawn, than willingly flow from thee. Be sparing in reporting improbable truths, especially to the vulgar, who, instead of informing their judgments will suspect thy credit. Disdain their peevish pride who rail on their native land (whose worst fault is that it bred such ungrateful fools,) and in all their discourses prefer foreign countries.

OF COMPANY.

Company is one of the greatest pleasures of the nature of man. For the beams of joy are made better by reflection, when related to another; and otherwise gladness itself must grieve for want of one to express itself to.

It is unnatural for a man to court and hug solitariness. It is observed, that the furthest islands in the world are so seated that there is none so remote but that from some shore of it another island or continent may be discerned; as if hereby nature invited countries to a mutual commerce one with another. Why then should any man affect to environ himself with so deep and great reservedness, as not to communicate with the society of others? And though we pity those who made solitariness their refuge in time of persecution, we must condemn such as choose it in the church's prosperity. For well may we count him not well in his wits, who will live always under a bush, because others in a storm shelter themselves under it.

Better therefore ride alone than have a thief's company. And such is a wicked man who will rob thee of precious time, if he doth no more mischief. We must not only avoid sin itself, but also the causes and occasions thereof: amongst which bad company (the lime-twigs of the devil) is the chiefest, especially to catch those natures which, like the good-fellow planet, Mercury, are most swayed by others.

If thou beest cast into bad company, like Hercules thou must sleep with thy club in thine hand, and stand on thy guard. I mean if against thy will the tempest of an unexpected occasion drives thee amongst such rocks; though with them, be not of them; keep civil communion with them, but separate from their sins, and if against thy will thou fallest amongst wicked men, know to thy comfort thou art still in thy calling, and therefore in God's keeping, who on thy prayers will preserve thee.

The company he keeps is the comment by help whereof men expound the most close and mystical man; understanding him for one of the same religion, life, and manners with his associates. And though perchance he be not such a one, it is just he should be counted so for conversing with them.

He that eats cherries with noblemen, shall have his eyes spirted out with the stones. This outlandish proverb hath in it an English truth, that they who constantly converse with men far above their estates shall reap shame and loss thereby. If thou payest nothing they will count thee a sucker, no branch ; if in payments thou keepest pace with them, their long strides will soon tire thy short legs.

To affect always to be the best of the company argues a base disposition. Gold always worn in the same purse with silver loses both of the colour and weight ; and so to converse always with inferiors, degrades a man of his worth. Such there are that love to be the lords of the company, whilst the rest must be their tenants : as if bound by their lease to approve, praise and admire whatsoever they say. These, knowing the lowness of their parts, love to live with dwarfs, that they may seem proper men. To come amongst their equals, they count it an abridgment of their freedom, but to be with their betters, they deem it flat slavery.

It is excellent for one to have a library of scholars, especially if they be plain to be read. I mean of a communicative nature, whose discourses are as full as fluent, and their judgments as right as their tongues ready : such men's talk shall be thy lectures.

Of Apparel.

Clothes are for necessity; warm clothes for health; cleanly for decency; lasting for thrift, and rich for magnificence. Now there may be a fault in their number, if too various; making, if too vain; matter, if too costly, and mind of the wearer, if he takes pride therein. We come therefore to some general directions.

It is a chargeable vanity to be constantly clothed above one's purse or place. I say constantly; for perchance sometimes it may be dispensed with. A great man, who himself was very plain in apparel, checked a gentleman for being over fine; who modestly answered, *Your lordship hath better clothes at home, and I have worse.* But sure no plea can be made when this luxury is grown to be ordinary.

It is beneath a wise man always to wear clothes beneath men of his rank. True there is a state sometimes in decent plainness. When a wealthy lord at a great solemnity had the plainest apparel; *O,* said one, *if you had marked it well, his suit had the richest pockets.* Yet it argues no wisdom in clothes always to stoop beneath his condition. When Antisthenes saw Socrates in a torn coat, he showed a hole thereof to the people : *and lo*, quoth he, *through this I see Socrates his pride.*

He shows a light gravity who loves to be an exception from a general fashion. For the received custom in the place where we live is the most competent judge of decency ; from which we must not appeal to our own opinion. When the French courtiers, mourning for their king, Henry the Second, had worn cloth a whole year, all silks became so vile in every man's eyes, that if any was seen to wear them, he was presently accounted a mechanic or country fellow.

To conclude, sumptuary laws in this land to reduce apparel to a set standard of price and fashion, according to the several states of men, have long been wished, but are little to be hoped for. Some think private men's superfluity is a necessary evil in a state, the floating of fashions affording a standing maintenance to many thousands, who otherwise would be at a loss for a livelihood.

OF BUILDING.

He that alters an old house is tied as a translator to the original, and is confined to the fancy of the first builder. Such a man were unwise to pluck down good old building, to erect, perchance, worse new. But those that raise a new house from the ground are blameworthy if they make it not handsome, seeing to them method and confusion are both at a rate. In building we must respect situation, contrivance, receipt, strength, and beauty.

Of situation ; chiefly choose a wholesome air. For air is a dish one feeds on every minute, and therefore it need be good. Wherefore great men, who may build where they please, as poor men where they can, if herein they prefer their profit above their health, I refer them to their physicians to make them pay for it accordingly.

Wood and water are two staple commodities where they may be had. The former I confess hath made so much iron, that it must now be bought with the more silver ; and grows daily dearer. But it is as well pleasant as profitable to see a house cased with trees. The worst is, where a place is bald of wood, no art can make it a periwig.

Next, a pleasant prospect is to be respected. A medley view, such as water and land at Greenwich, best entertains the eyes, refreshing the wearied beholder with exchange of objects. Yet I know a more profitable prospect where the owner can only see his own land round about.

A fair entrance with an easy ascent gives a great grace to a building : where the hall is a preferment out of the court, the parlour out of the hall ; not as in some old buildings where the doors are so low pigmies must stoop, and the rooms so high that giants may stand upright.   But now we are come to contrivance.

Let not thy common rooms be several, nor thy several rooms be common.   The hall, which is a Pandocheum, ought to lie open, and so ought passages and stairs, provided that the whole house be not spent in paths.

Light, God's eldest daughter, is a principal beauty in a building : yet it shines not alike from all parts of heaven.   An east window welcomes the infant beams of the sun, before they are of strength to do any harm, and is offensive to none but a sluggard. A south window in summer is a chimney with a fire in it, and needs the screen of a curtain.   In a west window in summer time towards night, the sun grows low, and over familiar with more light than delight. A north window is best for butteries and cellars, where the beer will be sour for the sun's smiling on it. Thorough lights are best for rooms of entertainment, and windows on one side for dormitories.   As for receipt,

A house had better be too little for a day, than too great for a year. And it is easier borrowing of thy neighbour a brace of rooms for a night, than a bag of money for a twelvemonth. It is vain, therefore, to proportion the receipt to an extraordinary occasion, as those who by overbuilding their houses have dilapidated their lands, and their states have been pressed to death under the weight of their house.

As for strength, country houses must be substantives, able to stand of themselves, not like city buildings supported by their neighbours on either side. By strength we mean such as may resist weather and time, not invasion, castles being out of date in this peaceable age. As for the making of moats round about, it is questionable whether the fogs be not more unhealthful than the fish brings profit, or the water defence. Beauty remains behind as the last to be regarded, because houses are made to be lived in not looked on.

Let not the front look asquint on a stranger, but accost him right at his entrance. Uniformity also much pleaseth the eye; and it is observed that freestone, like a fair complexion, soon waxeth old, whilst brick keeps her beauty longest.

Let the office-houses observe the due distance from the mansion-house. Those are too familiar which presume to be of the same pile with it. The same may be said of stables and barns; without which a house is like a city without works, it can never hold out long.

Gardens are also to attend in their place. When God planted a garden eastward, He made *to grow out of the ground every tree pleasant to the sight, and good for food*. Sure He knew better what was proper to a garden than those who now-a-days therein only feed the eyes, and starve both taste and smell.

To conclude, in building rather believe any man than an artificer in his own art for matter of charges; not that they cannot, but will not be faithful. Should they tell thee all the cost at the first, it would blast a young builder in the budding, and therefore they soothe thee up till it has cost thee something to confute them. The spirit of building first possessed people after the flood, which then caused the confusion of languages, and since of the estate of many a man.

Of Anger.

Anger is one of the sinews of the soul; he that wants it hath a maimed mind. Nor is it good to converse with such as cannot be angry. This anger

G

is either heavenly, when one is offended for God ; or
hellish, when offended with God and goodness ; or
earthly, in temporal matters. Which earthly anger,
whereof we treat, may also be hellish, if for no cause,
no great cause, too hot, or too long.

Be not angry with any without a cause. If thou
beest, thou must not only, as the proverb saith, be
appeased without amends, having neither cost nor
damage given thee, but, as our Saviour saith, *be in
danger of the judgment.*

Be not mortally angry with any for a venial fault.
He will make a strange combustion in the state of his
soul, who at the landing of every cockboat sets the
beacons on fire. To be angry for every toy debases
the worth of thy anger; for he will be angry for
anything who will be angry for nothing.

Let not thy anger be so hot, but that the most
torrid zone thereof may be habitable. Fright not
people from thy presence with the terror of thy in-
tolerable impatience. Some men, like a tiled house,
are long before they take fire, but once on flame there
is no coming near to quench them.

Take heed of doing irrevocable acts in thy passion,
as the revealing of secrets, which makes thee a bankrupt for society ever after ; neither do such things
which done once are done for ever, so that no bemoan-

ing can amend them : do not in an instant what an age cannot recompense.

St. Paul saith, *Let not the sun go down on your wrath :*[1] to carry news to the antipodes in another world of thy revengeful nature. Yet let us take the apostle's meaning rather than his words, with all possible speed to depose our passion, not understanding him so literally that we may take leave to be angry till sunset : then might our wrath lengthen with the days ; and men in Greenland, where day lasts above a quarter of a year, have plentiful scope of revenge. And as the English, by command from William the Conqueror, always raked up their fire and put out their candles when the curfew bell was rung. let us then also quench all sparks of anger and heats of passion.

He *that keeps anger long in his bosom, giveth place to the devil.*[2] And why should we make room for him, who will crowd in too fast of himself? Heat of passion makes our soul to chap, and the devil creeps in at the crannies ; yea, a furious man in his fits may seem possessed with a devil, foams, fumes, tears himself, is deaf and dumb, in effect, to hear or speak reason. Sometimes swallows, stares, stamps, with

---

[1] Ephes. iv. 26.   [2] Ephes. iv. 27.

fiery eyes and flaming cheeks. Had Narcissus himself
seen his own face when he had been angry, he could
never have fallen in love with himself.

OF MEMORY.

It is the treasure-house of the mind, wherein the
monuments thereof are kept and preserved. Plato
makes it the mother of the muses; Aristotle sets it
one degree further, making experience the mother of
arts, memory the parent of experience.

Artificial memory is rather a trick than an art, and
more for the gain of the teacher than profit of the
learners.

First soundly infix in thy mind what thou desirest
to remember. What wonder is it if agitation of
business jog that out of thy head, which was there
rather tacked than fastened? Whereas those notions
which get in by *violenta possessio* will abide there, till
ejectio firma, sickness or extreme age, dispossess them.
It is best knocking in the nail over-night, and clinching
it the next morning.

Overburthen not thy memory, to make so faithful
a servant a slave. Remember Atlas was weary.
Have as much reason as a camel, to rise when thou

hast thy full load. Memory, like a purse, if it be over-full that it cannot shut, all will drop out of it. Take heed of a gluttonous curiosity to feed on many things, lest the greediness of the appetite of thy memory spoil the digestion thereof. Beza's case was peculiar and memorable; being above fourscore years of age he perfectly could say by heart any Greek chapter in St. Paul's epistles[1] or anything else which he had learnt long before, but forgot whatsoever was newly told him; his memory, like an inn, retaining old guests, but having no room to entertain new. Spoil not thy memory with thine own jealousy nor make it bad by suspecting it. How canst thou find that true which thou wilt not trust? St. Augustine tells us of his friend Simplicius, who, being asked, could tell all Virgil's verses backward and forward; and yet the same party vowed to God that he knew not he could do it till they did try him. Sure there is concealed strength in men's memories which they take no notice of. Marshal thy notions into a handsome method. One will carry twice more weight trussed and packed up in bundles, than when it lies untowardly flapping and hanging about his shoulders. Things orderly fardled up under heads are most portable.

[1] Thuan., "Obit. Doct. Virorum," p. 384.

Adventure not all thy learning in one bottom, but divide it betwixt thy memory and thy note-books. He that with Bias carries all his learning about him in his head, will utterly be beggared and bankrupt, if a violent disease, a merciless thief, should rob and strip him. I know some have a common-place against common-place books, and yet perchance will privately make use of what publicly they declare against. A common-place book contains many notions in garrison, where the owner may draw out an army into the field on competent warning. Moderate diet and good air preserve memory; but what air is best I dare not define, when such great ones differ. Some say a pure and subtle air is best; another commends a thick and foggy air. For the Pisans, sited in the fens and marsh of Arnus, have excellent memories, as if the foggy air were a cap for their heads.

Thankfulness to God for it continues the memory: whereas some proud people have been visited with such oblivion that they have forgotten their own names. Staupitius, tutor to Luther, and a godly man, in a vain ostentation of his memory repeated Christ's genealogy (Matt. i.) by heart in his sermon, but being out about the captivity of Babylon, *I see,* saith he, *God resisteth the proud,* and so betook himself to his book.

OF FANCY.

It is an inward sense of the soul, for a while retaining and examining things brought in thither by the common sense. It is the most boundless and restless faculty of the soul, for whilst the understanding and the will are kept as it were in *libera custodia* to their objects of *verum et bonum*, the fancy is free from all engagements: it digs without a spade, sails without a ship, flies without wings, builds without charges, fights without bloodshed, in a moment striding from the centre to the circumference of the world, by a kind of omnipotency creating and annihilating things in an instant, and things divorced in nature are married in fancy as in a lawful place. It is also most restless; whilst the senses are bound, and reason in a manner asleep, fancy, like a sentinel, walks the round, ever working never wearied. The chief diseases of the fancy are, either that they are too wild and soaring, or else too low and grovelling: Of the first:

1. If thy fancy be but a little too rank, age itself will correct it. To lift too high is no fault in a young horse, because with travelling he will mend it for his own ease. Thus lofty fancies in young men will come

down of themselves, and in process of time the over-
plus will shrink to be but even measure. But if this
will not do it, then observe these rules.

2. Take part always with thy judgment against thy
fancy in any thing wherein they shall dissent. If thou
suspectest thy conceits too luxuriant, herein account
thy suspicion a legal conviction, and damn whatsoever
thou doubtest of.

3. Take the advice of a faithful friend, and submit
thy inventions to his censure. When thou pennest an
oration, let him have the power of *index expurgatorius*,
to expunge what he pleaseth. Mark the arguments
and reasons of his alterations ; why *that* phrase least
proper, *this* passage more cautious and advised ; and
after a while thou shalt perform the place in thine own
person, and not go out of thyself for a censurer. If
thy fancy be too low and humble,

4. Let thy judgment be king, but not tyrant over
it, to condemn harmless, yea, commendable conceits.
Some for fear their orations should giggle, will not let
them smile. Give it also liberty to rove, for it will not be
extravagant. There is no danger that weak folks, if they
walk abroad, will straggle far, as wanting strength.

5. Acquaint thyself with reading poets, for there
fancy is in her throne : and, in time, the sparks of the
author's wit will catch hold on the reader, and

inflame him with love, liking, and desire of imitation. I confess there is more required to teach one to write than to see a copy : however there is a secret force of fascination in reading poems to raise and provoke fancy. If thy fancy be over voluble, then

6. Whip this vagrant home to the first object whereon it should be settled. Indeed, nimbleness is the perfection of this faculty, but levity the bane of it. Great is the difference betwixt a swift horse and a skittish, that will stand on no ground. Such is the ubiquitary fancy, which will keep long residence on no one subject, but is so courteous to strangers, that it ever welcomes that conceit most which comes last ; and new species supplant the old ones, before seriously considered. If this be the fault of thy fancy, I say whip it home to the first object whereon it should be settled. This do as often as occasion requires, and by degrees the fugitive servant will learn to abide by his work without running away.

7. Acquaint thyself by degrees with hard and knotty studies, as school-divinity, which will clog thy over nimble fancy. True, at first it will be as welcome to thee as a prison, and their very solutions will seem knots unto thee. But take not too much at once, lest thy brain turn edge. Taste it first as a potion for physic, and by degrees thou shalt drink it as beer for

thirst : practice will make it pleasant. Mathematics are also good for this purpose. If beginning to try a conclusion, thou must make an end, lest thou lose thy pains that are past, and must proceed seriously and exactly.

8. To clothe low-creeping matter with high-flown language is not fine fancy, but flat foolery. It rather loads than raises a wren, to fasten the feathers of an ostrich to her wings. Some men's speeches are like the high mountains in Ireland, having a dirty bog in the top of them : the very ridge of them in high words having nothing of worth, but what rather stalls than delights the auditor.

9. Fine fancies in manufactures invent engines rather pretty than useful : and commonly one trade is too narrow for them. They are better to project new ways than to prosecute old, and are rather skilful in many mysteries than thriving in one. They affect not voluminous inventions, wherein many years must constantly be spent to perfect them, except there be in them variety of pleasant employment.

10. Imagination, the work of the fancy, hath produced real effects. Many serious and sad examples hereof may be produced : I will only insist on a merry one. A gentleman having led a company of children beyond their usual journey, they began to be weary,

and jointly cried to him to carry them ; which because of their multitude, he could not do, but told them he would provide them horses to ride on. Then cutting little wands out of the hedge as nags for them, and a great stake as a gelding for himself, thus mounted, fancy put metal into their legs, and they came cheerfully home.

11. Fancy runs most furiously when a guilty conscience drives it. One that owed much money and had many creditors, as he walked London streets in the evening, a tenter-hook caught his cloak. *At whose suit?* said he, conceiving some bailiff had arrested him. Thus guilty consciences are afraid where no fear is, and count every creature they meet a serjeant sent from God to punish them.

OF RECREATIONS.

Recreations. A second creation, when weariness hath almost annihilated one's spirits. The breathing of the soul, which otherwise would be stifled with continual business. We may trespass in them, if using such as are forbidden by the lawyer, as against the statutes ; physician, as against health ; divine, as against conscience.

Be well satisfied in thy conscience of the lawfulness of the recreation thou usest. He that sins against his conscience sins with a witness.

Spill not the morning (the quintessence of the day) in recreations. For sleep itself is a recreation; add not therefore sauce to sauce; and he cannot properly have any title to be refreshed who was not first faint. Pastime, like wine, is poison in the morning. It is then good husbandry to sow the head, which hath lain fallow all night, with some serious work. Chiefly entrench not on the Lord's day to use unlawful sports; this were to spare thine own flock and to shear God's lamb.

Let thy recreations be ingenious, and bear proportion with thine age. If thou sayest with Paul, *When I was a child, I did as a child;* say also with him, *but when I was a man, I put away childish things.* Wear also the child's coat if thou usest his sports.

Take heed also of boisterous and over violent exercises. Ringing ofttimes hath made good music on the bells, and put men's bodies out of tune, so that by over-heating themselves they have rung their own passing-bell.

Yet the ruder sort of people scarce count anything a sport which is not loud and violent. The Muscovite women esteem none loving husbands, except they beat their wives. It is no pastime with country clowns that cracks not pates, breaks not shins, bruises not limbs, tumbles and tosses not all the body.

Refresh that part of thyself which is most wearied. If thy life be sedentary, exercise thy body; if stirring and active, recreate thy mind. But take heed of cozening thy mind, in setting it to do a double task under pretence of giving it a play-day, as in the labyrinth of chess, and other tedious and studious games.

Yet recreations distasteful to some dispositions, relish best to others. Fishing with an angle is to some rather a torture than a pleasure, to stand an hour as mute as the fish they mean to take. As soon may the same meat please all palates, as the same sport suit all dispositions.

Running, leaping, and dancing, the descants on the plain song of walking, are all excellent exercises. And yet those are the best recreations which, besides refreshing, enable, at least dispose men to some other good ends. Bowling teaches men's hands and eyes mathematics, and the rules of proportion: swimming hath saved many a man's life, when himself hath been both the wares and the ship: tilting and fencing is war without anger; and manly sports are the grammar of military performance. But above all, shooting is a noble recreation, and a half liberal art.

Choke not thy soul with immoderate pouring in the cordial of pleasures. Rather abridge thyself of thy lawful liberty herein. And then recreations shall both strengthen labour and sweeten rest, and we may expect God's blessing and protection on us in following them, as well as in doing our work : for he that saith grace for his meat, in it prays also to God to bless the sauce unto him. As for those that will not take lawful pleasure, I am afraid they will take unlawful pleasure, and by lacing themselves too hard grow awry on one side.

OF TOMBS.

Tombs are the clothes of the dead : a grave is but a plain suit, and a rich monument is one embroidered. Tombs ought in some sort to be proportioned, not to the wealth, but deserts of the party interred. Yet we may see some rich man of mean worth loaden under a tomb big enough for a prince to bear. There were officers appointed in the Grecian games, who always by public authority did pluck down the statues erected to the victors, if they exceeded the true symmetry and proportion of their bodies. We need such now-a-days to order monuments to men's merits. Over-costly tombs are only baits for sacrilege.

The shortest, plainest, and truest epitaphs are best. I say the shortest ; for when a passenger sees a chronicle written on a tomb, he takes it on trust some great man lies there buried, without taking pains to examine who he is. Mr. Camden, in his "Remains," presents us with examples of great men that had little epitaphs. And when once I asked a witty gentleman, an honoured friend of mine, what epitaph was fittest to be written on Mr. Camden's tomb? "Let it be," said he, "CAMDEN'S REMAINS." I say also the plainest, for except the sense be above ground, few will trouble themselves to dig for it. Lastly it must be true. Not as in some monuments, where the red veins in the marble may seem to blush at the falsehoods written on it. He was a witty man who first taught a stone to speak, but he was a wicked man that taught it first to lie.

A good memory is the best monument. Others are subject to casualty and time, and we know that the pyramids themselves, doting with age, have forgotten the names of their founders. To conclude let us be careful to provide rest for our souls, and our bodies will provide rest for themselves.

OF DEFORMITY.

Deformity is either natural, voluntary, or adventitious, being either caused by God's unseen providence, (by men nicknamed chance,) or by man's cruelty. We will take them in order.

If thou beest not so handsome as thou wouldest have been, thank God thou art no more unhandsome than thou art. It is His mercy thou art not the mark for passengers' fingers to point at, an heteroclite in nature, with some members defective or redundant. Be glad that thy clay cottage hath all the necessary rooms thereto belonging, though the outside be not so fairly plastered as some others.

Yet is it lawful and commendable by art to correct the defects and deformities of nature. Ericthonius being a goodly man from the girdle upwards, but as the poets feign, having downwards the body of a serpent (moralize him to have had some defect in his feet,) first invented chariots, wherein he so sat that the upper parts of him might be seen, and the rest of his body concealed.[1] Little heed is to be given to his

[1] Servius, in illud Virg. Georg. iii. " Primus Ericthonius," etc.

lying pen who maketh Anne Bullen, mother to Queen Elizabeth, the first finder out and wearer of ruffs, to cover a wen she had in her neck. Yet the matter is not much, such an addition of art being without any fraud or deceit.

Mock not at those who are misshapen by nature. There is the same reason of the poor and of the deformed; he that despiseth them, despiseth God that made them. A poor man is the picture of God's own making, but set in a plain frame, not gilded : a deformed man is also his workmanship, but not drawn with even lines and lively colours. The former, not for want of wealth, as for the latter not for want of skill, but both for the pleasure of the maker. As for Aristotle, who would have parents expose their deformed children to the wide world without caring for them, his opinion herein, not only deformed but most monstrous, deserves rather to be exposed to the scorn and contempt of all men.

Some people handsome by nature, have wilfully deformed themselves. Such as wear Bacchus his colours in their faces, arising not from having, but being bad livers.

Nature oftentimes recompenseth deformed bodies with excellent wits. Witness Æsop, than whose fables children cannot read an easier, nor men a wiser book ; for all latter moralists do but write comments upon them.

Their souls have been the chapels of sanctity, whose bodies have been the spitolls of deformity. An emperor of Germany coming by chance on a Sunday into a church, found there a misshapen priest, insomuch as the emperor scorned and contemned him. But when he heard him read those words in the service, *For it is he that made us, and not we ourselves*, the emperor checked his own proud thoughts, and made inquiry into the quality and condition of the man, and finding him on examination to be most learned and devout, he made him Archbishop of Cologne, which place he did excellently discharge.

Of Plantations.

Plantations make mankind broader, as generation makes it thicker. To advance a happy plantation, the undertakers, planters, and place itself must contribute their endeavours.

Let the prime undertakers be men of no shallow heads, nor narrow fortunes. Such as have a real estate, so that if defeated in their adventure abroad, they may have a retreating place at home, and such as will be contented with their present loss, to be benefactors to posterity.

Let the planters be honest, skilful, and painful people. For if they be such as leap thither from the gallows, can any hope for cream out of scum, when men send, as I may say, Christian savages to heathen savages? It was rather bitterly than falsely spoken concerning one of our western plantations, consisting most of dissolute people, *that it was very like unto England, as being spit out of the very mouth of it.* Nor must the planters be only honest, but industrious also. What hope is there that they who were drones at home will be bees abroad, especially if far off from any to oversee them.

Let the place be naturally strong, or at leastwise capable of fortification. For though at first planters are sufficiently fenced with their own poverty, and though at the beginning their worst enemies will spare them out of pity to themselves, their spoil not countervailing the cost of spoiling them ; yet when once they have gotten wealth, they must get strength to defend it. Here know, islands are easily shut, whereas continents have their doors ever open, not to be bolted without great charges. Besides, unadvised are those planters who, having choice of ground, have built their towns in places of a servile nature, as being overawed and constantly commanded by some hills about them.

Let it have a self-sufficiency, or some staple commodity to balance traffic with other countries. As for a self-sufficiency, few countries can stand alone. Staple commodities are such as are never out of fashion, as belonging to a man's being; being with comfort, being with delight, the luxury of our age having made superfluities necessary. And such a place will thrive the better, when men may say with Isaac, *Rehoboth; Now the Lord hath made room for us,*[1] when new colonies come not in with extirpation of the natives; for this is rather a supplanting than a planting.

Let the planters labour to be loved and feared of the natives. With whom let them use all just bargaining: keeping all covenants, performing all promises with them: let them embrace all occasions to convert them, knowing that each convert is a conquest: and it is more honour to overcome paganism in one, than to conquer a thousand pagans. As for the inscription of a Deity in their hearts, it need not be new written but only new scoured in them.

[1] Gen. xxvi. 22.

Of Contentment.

It is one property which, they say, is required of those who seek for the philosopher's stone, that they must not do it with any covetous desire to be rich; for otherwise they shall never find it. But most true it is that whosoever would have the jewel of contentment, which turns all into gold, yea want into wealth, must come with minds divested of all ambitious and covetous thoughts, else are they never likely to obtain it. We will describe contentment first negatively.

It is not a senseless stupidity what becomes of our outward estates. God would have us take notice of all accidents which from him happen to us in worldly matters. Had the martyrs had the dead palsy before they went to the stake to be burnt, their sufferings had not been so glorious. It is not a word-braving, or scorning of all wealth in discourse. Generally those who boast most of contentment have least of it. Their very boasting shows that they want something, and basely beg it, namely commendation.

But it is a humble and willing submitting ourselves to God's pleasure in all conditions. One observeth (how truly I dispute not) that the French naturally

have so elegant and graceful a carriage, that what
posture of body soever in their salutations, or what
fashion of attire soever they are pleased to take on
them, it doth so beseem them, that one would think
nothing can become them better. Thus contentment
makes men carry themselves gracefully in wealth,
want, in health, sickness, freedom, fetters, yea what
condition soever God allots them.

It is no breach of contentment for men to complain that their sufferings are unjust, as offered by
men : provided they allow them for just, as proceed-
ing from God, who useth wicked men's injustice to
correct his children. But let us take heed that we
bite not so high at the handle of the rod, as to
fasten on his hand that holds it ; our discontentments
mounting so high as to quarrel with God himself.

It is no breach of contentment for men by lawful
means to seek the removal of their misery, and better-
ing of their estate. Thus men ought by industry
to endeavour the getting of more wealth, ever submitting themselves to God's will. A lazy hand is no
argument of a contented heart. God's spirit is the
best schoolmaster to teach contentment : a schoolmaster who can make good scholars, and warrant the
success as well as his endeavour; the school of sanctified
afflictions is the best place to learn contentment in :

I say sanctified ; for naturally, like restive horses, we go the worse for the beating, if God bless not afflictions unto us.   Contentment consisteth not in adding more fuel, but in taking away some fire; not in multiplying of wealth, but in subtracting men's desires.   He that at first thought ten thousand pounds too much for any one man, will afterward think ten millions too little for himself.

Men create more discontents to themselves, than ever happened to them for others.   *Man disquieteth himself in vain*, with many causeless and needless afflictions.

Pious meditations much advantage contentment in adversity.   Such as these are, to consider first, that more are beneath us than above us ; secondly, many of God's dear saints have been in the same condition; thirdly, we want rather superfluities than necessities ; fourthly, the more we have the more we must account for ; earthly blessings, through man's corruptions, are more prone to be abused than well used.

We must leave all earthly wealth at our death, and *riches avail not in the day of wrath*.   But as some use to fill up the stamp of light gold with dirt, thereby to make it weigh the heavier, so it seems some men load their souls with thick clay to make them pass the better in God's balance, but all to no

purpose. The less we have, the less it will grieve us
to leave this world; lastly it is the will of God, and
therefore both for His glory and our good, whereof we
ought to be assured. I have heard how a gentleman,
travelling in a misty morning, asked of a shepherd
(such men being generally skilled in the physiognomy
of the heavens) what weather it would be? *It will be,*
said the shepherd, *what weather shall please me;* and
being courteously requested to express his meaning:
Sir, saith he, *it shall be what weather pleaseth God,
and what weather pleaseth God pleaseth me.* Thus
contentment maketh men to have even what they
think fitting themselves, because submitting to God's
will and pleasure.

To conclude, a man ought to be like unto a cunning
actor, who, if he be enjoined to represent the person
of some prince or nobleman, does it with a grace and
comeliness; if by and by he be commanded to lay
that aside, and play the beggar, he does that as
willingly and as well.

OF BOOKS.

Solomon saith truly, *Of making many books there is
no end,* so insatiable is the thirst of men therein: as

also endless is the desire of many buying and reading them. But we come to our rules.

It is a vanity to persuade the world one hath much learning, by getting a great library. As soon shall I believe everyone is valiant that hath a well-furnished armoury. I guess good housekeeping by the smoking, not the number of the tunnels, as knowing that many of them, built merely for uniformity, are without chimneys, and more without fires. Few books, well selected, are best. Yet, as a certain fool bought all the pictures that came out, because he might have his choice, such is the vain humour of many men in gathering of books.

Some books are only cursorily to be tasted of. Namely, first, voluminous books, the task of a man's life to read them over; secondly, auxiliary books, only to be repaired to on occasions; thirdly, such as are mere pieces of formality, so that if you look on them, you look through them; and he that peeps through the casement of the index, sees as much as if he were in the house. But the laziness of those cannot be excused who perfunctorily pass over authors of consequence, and only trade in their tables and contents. These like city-cheaters, having gotten the names of all country gentlemen, make silly people believe they have long lived in those places where they never were, and flourish with skill in those authors they never seriously studied.

The genius of the author is commonly discovered in the dedicatory epistle. Many place the purest grain in the mouth of the sack for the chapman to handle or buy : and from the dedication one may probably guess at the work, saving some rare and peculiar exceptions. Thus, when once a gentleman admired how so pithy, learned, and witty a dedication was matched to a flat, dull, foolish book : *In truth,* saith another, *they may be well matched together, for I profess they are nothing akin.*

Proportion an hour's meditation to an hour's reading of a staple author. This makes a man master of his learning, and dispirits the book into the scholar. The king of Sweden never filed his men above six deep in one company, because he would not have them lie in useless clusters in his army, but so that every particular soldier might be drawn out into service. Books that stand thin on the shelves, yet so as the owner of them can bring forth every one of them into use, are better than far greater libraries.

Learning hath gained most by those books by which the printers have lost. Arius Montanus, in printing the Hebrew Bible, commonly called the Bible of the king of Spain, much wasted himself, and was accused in the court of Rome for his good deed. Likewise Christopher Plantin, by printing of his curious interlineary Bible, in Antwerp, through the unseasonable exactions of the king's officers, sunk and almost ruined his estate. And our worthy English knight, who set forth the golden-mouthed father in a silver print, was a loser by it.

Whereas foolish pamphlets prove most beneficial to the printers. When a French printer complained that he was utterly undone by printing a solid serious book of Rabelais concerning physic, Rabelais, to make him recompense, made that his jesting scurrilous work, which repaired the printer's loss with advantage. Such books the world swarms too much with. When one had set out a witless pamphlet, writing *finis* at the end thereof, another wittily wrote beneath it,

> " *Nay there thou liest, my friend,*
> *In writing foolish books there is no End."*

And surely such scurrilous scandalous papers do more than conceivable mischief. First, their lusciousness puts many palates out of taste, that they can never after relish any solid and wholesome writers ; secondly, they cast dirt on the faces of many innocent persons, which dried on by continuance of time can never after be washed off; thirdly, the pamphlets of this age may pass for records with the next, because publicly uncontrolled, and what we laugh at, our children may believe ; fourthly, grant the things true they jeer at, yet this music is unlawful in any Christian church, to play upon the sins and miseries of others, the fitter object of the elegies than the satires of all truly religious.

But what do I speaking against multiplicity of books in this age, who trespass in this nature myself?

OF TIME-SERVING.

There be four kinds of time-serving : first, out of Christian discretion, which is commendable; second, out of human infirmity, which is more pardonable ; third, and fourth, out of ignorance, or affectation, both of which are damnable : of them in order.

He is a good time-server that complies his manners to the several ages of this life. He is a good time-server that finds out the fittest opportunity for every action. God hath made *a time for every thing under the sun*, save only for that which we do at all times, to wit, sin.

He is a good time-server that improves the present for God's glory and his own salvation. Of all the extent of time only the instant is that which we can call ours.

He is a good time-server that is pliant to the times in matters of mere indifferency. To blame are they whose minds may seem to be made of one entire bone, without any joints : they cannot bend at all, but stand as stiffly in things of pure indifferency, as in matters of absolute necessity.

He is a good time-server that in time of persecution neither betrays God's cause, nor his own safety.

Some have served the times out of mere ignorance. Gaping, for company, as others gaped before them, *Pater noster*, or, Our Father. I could both sigh and smile at the witty simplicity of a poor old woman who had lived in the days of Queen Mary and Queen Elizabeth, and said her prayers daily both in Latin and English; and *Let God*, said she, *take to himself which he likes best*.

But worst are those who serve the times out of mere affectation. Doing as the times do, not because the times do as they should do, but merely for sinister respects, to ingratiate themselves.

It is a very difficult thing to serve the times ; they change so frequently, so suddenly, and sometimes so violently from one extreme to another. The times under Diocletian were pagan ; under Constantine,

Christian; under Constantius, Arian; under Julian, apostate; under Jovian, Christian again, and all within the age of man, the term of seventy years. And would it not have wrenched and sprained his soul with short turning, who in all these should have been of the religion *for the time being.*

Time-servers are oftentimes left in the lurch. If they do not only give their word for the times in their constant discourses, but also give their bonds for them, and write in their defence. Such, when the times turn afterwards to another extreme, are left in the briars, and come off very hardly from the bill of their hands: if they turn again with the times, none will trust them; for who will make a staff of an osier?[1]

Miserable will be the condition of such time-servers when their master is taken from them. When as the angel swore (Rev. x. 6) that *time shall be no longer.* Therefore it is best serving of Him who is eternity, a master that can ever protect us.

To conclude, he that intends to meet with one in a great fair, and knows not where he is, may sooner find him by standing still in some principal place there, than by traversing it up and down. Take thy stand on some good ground in religion, and keep thy

---

[1] Lord Bacon, in " Henry Seventh," p. 211.

station in a fixed posture, never hunting after the times to follow them, and a hundred to one they will come to thee once in thy life time.

OF MODERATION.

Moderation is the silken string running through the pearl chain of all virtues,[1] it appears both in practice and judgment: we will insist on the latter, and describe it first negatively.

Moderation is not a halting betwixt two opinions, when the thorough believing of one of them is necessary to salvation : no pity is to be shown to such voluntary cripples. We read (Acts xxvii. 12) of a haven in Crete *which lay towards the south-west, and* towards the *north-west*, strange, that it could have part of two opposite points, north and south : sure it must be very winding. And thus some men's souls are in such intricate postures, they lay towards the papists and towards the protestants ; such we count not of moderate judgment, but of an immoderate unsettledness.

Nor is it a lukewarmness in those things wherein

[1] Bishop Hall, " Of Christian Moderation," p. 6.

God's glory is concerned. But it is a mixture of discretion and charity in one's judgment. Discretion puts a difference betwixt things absolutely necessary to salvation to be done and believed, and those which are of a second sort and lower form, wherein more liberty and latitude is allowed. In maintaining whereof, the stiffness of the judgment is abated, and suppled with charity towards his neighbour. The lukewarm man sees only his own ends, and particular profit ; the moderate man aims at the good of others, and unity of the church.

Yet such moderate men are commonly crushed betwixt the extreme parties on both sides. But what said Ignatius ? *I am Christ's wheat, and must be ground with the teeth of beasts, that I may be made God's pure manchet.* Saints are born to suffer, and must take it patiently. Besides in this world generally they get the least preferment ; it faring with them as with the guest that sat in the midst of the table, who could reach to neither mess, above or beneath him :

"Both ends of the table furnish'd are with meat,
Whilst they in middle nothing have to eat.
They were none of the wisest well I wist,
Who make bliss in the middle to consist."

Yet these temporal inconveniences of moderation are

abundantly recompensed with other better benefits, for a well informed judgment in itself is a preferment.

As the moderate man's temporal hopes are not great, so his fears are the less. He fears not to have the splinters of his party, when it breaks, fly into his eyes, or to be buried under the ruins of his side, if suppressed. He never pinned his religion on any man's sleeve, no not on the arm of flesh, and therefore is free from all dangerous engagements. His conscience is clear from raising schisms in the church.

His religion is more constant and durable; being here, *in via* in his way to heaven, and jogging on a good traveller's pace he overtakes and outgoes many violent men, whose over-hot ill-grounded zeal was quickly tired.

In matters of moment, indeed, none are more zealous. He thriftily treasures up his spirits for that time, who if he had formerly rent his lungs for every trifle, he would have wanted breath in points of importance.

Once in an age the moderate man is in the fashion, each extreme courts him to make them friends; and surely he hath a great advantage to be a peacemaker betwixt opposite parties. Now whilst, as we have said, moderate men are constant to themselves, violent men reel from one extremity to another.

I

As the world is round, so we may observe a circulation in opinions, and violent men turn often round in their tenets.

Pride is the greatest enemy to moderation. This makes men stickle for their opinions, to make them fundamental : proud men, having deeply studied some additional point in divinity, will strive to make the same necessary to salvation, to enhance the value of their own worth and pains ; and it must be fundamental in religion, because it is fundamental to their reputation. Yea, as love doth descend, and men dote most on their grandchildren, so these are indulgent to the deductions of their deductions, and consequential inferences, to the seventh generation, making them all of the foundation, though scarce of the building of religion. Next to pride, popular applause is the greatest foe moderation hath, and sure they who sail with that wind have their own vain-glory for their haven.

To close up all, let men, on God's blessing, soundly yet wisely, whip and lash lukewarmness and time-serving, their throngs will never fly in the face of true moderation, to do it any harm.

OF GRAVITY.

Gravity is the ballast of the soul, which keeps the mind steady.   It is either true or counterfeit.

Natural dulness, and heaviness of temper, is sometimes mistaken for true gravity : in such men, in whose constitutions one of the retrarch elements, *fire*, may seem to be omitted.   These sometimes not only cover their defects, but get praise.   They do wisely to counterfeit a reservedness, and to keep their chests always locked, not for fear any should steal treasure thence, but lest some should look in and see that there is nothing within them.   Wonder not so much that such men are grave, but wonder at them if they be not grave.

Affected gravity passes often for that which is true : I mean with dull eyes, for in itself nothing is more ridiculous.   When one shall use the preface of a mile to bring in a furlong of matter, set his face and speech in a frame, and to make men believe it is some precious liquor, their words come out drop by drop : such men's visards do sometimes fall from them, not without the laughter of the beholders.   One was called *gravity* for his affected solemnness, who afterwards being catched in a light prank, was ever after to the day of his death called *gravity-levity*.

True gravity expresses itself in gait, gesture, apparel, and speech. As for speech, gravity enjoins it ; not to be over much. *In the multitude of words there wanteth not sin.*[1] For of necessity many of them must be idle, whose best commendation is that they are good for nothing. Great talkers discharge too thick to take always true aim ; besides it is odious in a company. A man full of words who took himself to be a grand wit, made his brag that he was the leader of the discourse in what company soever he came, and *None*, said he, *dare speak in my presence if I hold my peace. No wonder*, answered one, *for they are all struck dumb at the miracle of your silence.*

To be wise and discreet : (Colossians iv. 6) *Let your speech be alway with grace, seasoned with salt. Always* not only sometimes, in the company of godly men. Tindal's being in the room, hindered a juggler, that he could not play his feats :[2] a saint's presence stops the devil's elbow-room to do his tricks ; and so some wicked men are awed into good discourse whilst pious people are present. But it must be always *seasoned with salt*, which is the *primum vivens et ulti-*

[1] Prov. x. 19.   [2] Fox's " Martyrs," p. 1079.

mum moriens at a feast, first brought and last taken away, and set in the midst as most necessary there-unto: *with salt*, that is, with wisdom and discretion, *non salibus, sed sale ;* nor yet with smarting jeers, like those whose discourse is fire-salt, speaking constant satires to the disgrace of others.

That may be done privately without breach of gravity, which may not be done publicly. As when a father makes himself his child's rattle, sporting with him till the father hath devoured the wise man in him. Making play unto him, that one would think he killed his own discretion to bring his child asleep. Such cases are no trespass on gravity, and married men may claim their privilege *to be judged by their peers*, and may herein appeal from the censuring verdict of bachelors.

Nature in men is sometimes unjustly taxed for a trespass against gravity. Some have active spirits, yea their ordinary pace is a race. Others have so scornful a carriage, that he who seeth them once may think them to be all pride, whilst he that seeth them often knows them to have none. Others have, per-chance, a misbeseeming garb in gesture, which they cannot amend ; that fork needing strong tines where-with one must thrust away nature. A fourth sort are of a merry cheerful disposition ; and God forbid all such should be condemned for lightness! O let not any envious eye disinherit men of that which is their *portion in this life ;*[1] comfortably to enjoy the blessings thereof. Yet gravity must prune, though not root out our mirth.

God alone is the giver of true gravity. No man wants so much of any grace as he hath to spare, and a constant impression of God's omnipresence is an excellent way to fix men's souls.

OF MARRIAGE.

Though bachelors be the strongest stakes, married men are the best binders in the hedge of the commonwealth. It is the policy of the Londoners, when they send a ship into the Levant or Mediterranean sea to make every mariner therein a merchant, each seaman adventuring somewhat of his own, which will make him more wary to avoid, and more valiant to undergo dangers. Thus married men, especially if having posterity, are the deeper sharers in that state wherein they live, which engageth their affections to the greater loyalty.

It is the worst clandestine marriage when God is

[1] Eccles. vii. 18.

not invited to it. Wherefore beforehand beg his gracious assistance. Marriage shall prove no lottery to thee, when the hand of Providence chooseth for thee, who if drawing a blank, can turn it into a prize, by sanctifying a bad wife unto thee.

Deceive not thyself by over expecting happiness in the married estate. Look not therein for content-ment greater than God will give, or a creature in this world can receive, namely, to be free from all incon-veniences. Marriage is not like the hill Olympus, wholly clear, without clouds; yea expect both wind and storm sometimes, which when blown over, the air is clearer and wholesomer for it. Yet all the molesta-tions of marriage are abundantly recompensed with other comforts which God bestoweth on them who make a wise choice of a wife, and observe the following rules.

Let grace and goodness be the principal loadstone of thy affections. For love which hath ends will have an end; whereas that which is founded on true virtue will always continue.

Neither choose all, nor not at all for beauty. A cried-up beauty makes more for her own praise than her husband's profit. They tell us of a floating island in Scotland: but sure no wise pilot will cast anchor there, lest the land swim away with his ship. So are they served, and justly enough, who only fasten their love on fading beauty, and both fail together.

Let there be no great disproportion in age. They that marry ancient people merely in expectation to bury them, hang themselves in hope that one will come and cut the halter. Let wealth in its due distance be regarded. Parents for a little pelf often marry their children to those whose persons they hate.

This shall serve for a conclusion. A bachelor was saying, *Next to no wife, a good wife is best*. *Nay*, said a gentlewoman, *next to a good wife, no wife is the best*. I wish to all married people the outward happiness which (anno 1605) happened to a couple in the city of Delpht, in Holland, living most lovingly together seventy-five years in wedlock, till the man being one hundred and three, the woman ninety-nine years of age, died within three hours each of other, and were buried in the same grave.

OF FAME.

Fame is the echo of actions, resounding them to the world, save that the echo repeats only the last part, but fame relates all, and often more than all.

Fame sometimes hath created something out of nothing. She hath made whole countries more than ever nature did, especially near the poles, and then hath peopled them likewise with inhabitants of her own invention, pigmies, giants, and amazons : yea fame is sometimes like unto a kind of mushroom, which Pliny recounts to be the greatest miracle in nature, because growing and having no root, as fame no ground of her reports.

Fame often makes a great deal of a little. Absalom killed one of David's sons, and fame killed all the rest ;[1] and generally she magnifies and multiplies matters.

Some fames are most difficult to trace to their form : and those who have sought to track them, have gone rather in a circle than forward, and oftentimes, through the doubling of reports, have returned back again where they began.

Politicians sometimes raise fames on purpose. As that such things are done already, which they mean to do afterwards. By the light of those false fires they see into men's hearts, and these false rumours are true scouts to discover men's dispositions. Besides, the deed, though strange in itself, is done

[1] 2 Sam. xiii. 30.

afterward with the less noise, men having vented their wonder beforehand, and the strangeness of the action is abated, because formerly made stale in report. But if the rumour startles men extremely, and draws with it dangerous consequences, then they can presently confute it, let their intentions fall, and prosecute it no further.

Incredible is the swiftness of fame in carrying reports. First she creeps through a village ; then she goes through a town; then she runs through a city ; then she flies through a country : still the farther the faster. General reports are seldom false. *Vox populi vox Dei.* A body of that greatness hath an eye of like clearness, and it is impossible that a wanderer with a counterfeit pass should pass undiscovered.

A fond fame is best confuted by neglecting it. By fond understand such a report as is rather ridiculous than dangerous if believed. It is not worth the making a schism betwixt newsmongers to set an antifame against it. Yea seriously and studiously to endeavour to confute it will grace the rumour too much, and give suspicion that, indeed, there is some reality in it. What madness were it to plant a piece of ordinance to beat down an aspen leaf, which having always the palsy will at last fall down of itself. And fame hath much of the scold in her; the best way to silence her is to be silent, and then at last she will be out of breath with blowing her own trumpet.

Fame sometimes reports things less than they are. Pardon her for offending herein, she is guilty so seldom. Fame generally overdoes, underdoes but in some particulars. The Italian proverb hath it, *There is less honesty, wisdom and money in men, than is counted on :* yet sometimes a close churl, who locks his coffers so fast fame could never peep into them, dieth richer than he was reported when alive. None could come near to feel his estate ; it might therefore cut fatter in his purse than was expected. But fame falls most short in those transcendents which are above her predicaments; as in Solomon's wisdom : *And behold one half was not told me ; thy wisdom and prosperity exceedeth the fame that I heard.*[1] But chiefly in forereporting the happiness in heaven, which eye hath not seen, nor ear heard, neither hath it entered into the heart of man to conceive.

[1] 1 Kings x. 7.

Of Ministers' Maintenance.

Maintenance of ministers ought to be plentiful, certain, and in some sort proportionable to their deserts. It should be plentiful, because

1. Their education was very chargeable to fit them for their profession, both at school and in the university : their books very dear, and those which they brought in folio, shrink quickly into quartos, in respect of the price their executors can get for them.

2. Because ministers are to subsist in a free, liberal and comfortable way. Oh, let not the ministers of the gospel be slaves to others, and servants to themselves ! They are not to pry into gain through every small chink. It becomes them rather to be acquainted with the nature of things, than with the prizes, and to know them rather as they are in the world, than as they are in the market. Otherwise, if his means be small, and living poor, necessity will bolt him out of his own study, and send him to the barn, when he should be at his book, or make him study his Easter book more than all other writers. Hereupon, some wanting what they should have at home, have done what they should not abroad.

3. Because hospitality is expected at their hands. The poor come to their houses as if they had interest in them, and the ministers can neither receive or refuse them. Not to relieve them, were not Christianity; and to relieve them, were worse than infidelity, because therein they wrong their providing for their own family. Thus sometimes they are forced to be Nabals against their will; yet it grieveth them to send the people away empty. But what shall they do, seeing they cannot multiply their loaves and their fishes?

4. Because they are to provide for their posterity that after the death of their parents they may live, · though not in a high yet in an honest fashion, neither leaving them to the wide world, nor a narrow cottage.

Ministers' maintenance ought to be certain; lest some of them meet with Labans for their patrons and parishioners; changing their wages ten times, and at last, if the fear of God doth not fright them, send them away empty.

What reason is it that whilst law and physic bring great portions to such as marry them, divinity, their elder sister, should only be put off with her own beauty; in after ages men will rather bind their sons to one gainful, than to seven liberal sciences : only the lowest of the people would be made ministers, which cannot otherwise subsist; and it would be bad when God's church is made a sanctuary only for men of desperate estates to take refuge in.

However, let every minister take up this resolution, *To preach the word, to be instant in season, out of season, reprove, rebuke, exhort with all long-suffering and doctrine.* If thou hast competent means comfortably to subsist on, be the more thankful to God, the fountain, to man, the channel; painful in thy place, pitiful to the poor, cheerful in spending some, careful in keeping the rest. If not, yet tire not for want of a spur, do something for love, and not all for money ; for love of God, of goodness, of the godly, of a good conscience. Know it is better to want means than to detain them; the one only suffers, the other deeply sins : and it is as dangerous a persecution to religion to draw the fuel from it, as to cast water on it. Comfort thyself that another world will pay this world's debts, *and great is thy reward with God in heaven.* A reward, in respect of his promise ; a gift, in respect of thy worthlessness: and yet the less thou lookest at it, the surer thou shalt find it, if labouring with thyself to serve God for himself, in respect of whom, even heaven itself is but a sinister end.

THE WISE STATESMAN.

To describe the statesman at large, is a subject rather of a volume than a chapter, and is as far beyond my power as wide of my profession. We will not launch out into the deep, but satisfy ourselves to sail by the shore, and briefly observe his carriage towards God, his king, himself, home persons, and foreign princes.

He counts the fear of God the beginning of wisdom; and therefore esteemeth no project profitable, which is not lawful; nothing politic, which crosseth piety. Let not any plead for the contrary Hushai's dealing with Absalom, which strongly savoured of double-dealing; for what is a question cannot be an argument, seeing the lawfulness of his deed therein was never decided; and he is unwise that will venture the state of his soul on the litigious title of such an example. Besides, we must live by God's precepts, not by the godliest practice. And though God causeth some-times the sun of success to shine as well on bad as good projects, yet commonly wicked actions end in shame at the last.

In giving counsel to his prince, he had rather displease than hurt him. Yet if dissenting from his sovereign, he doth it with all humility and moderation. He is constant, but not obstinate in the advice he gives. Some think it beneath a wise man to alter his opinion; a maxim both false and dangerous. We know what worthy father wrote his own retraction; and it matters not though we go back from our word, so we go forward in the truth and a sound judgment. Such a one changeth not his main opinion, which ever was this, to embrace that course which upon mature deliberation shall appear unto him the most advised.

As for his carriage towards himself, he taketh an exact survey of his own defects and perfections. As for the former, his weaknesses and infirmities he doth carefully and wisely conceal. His known perfections he seeks modestly to cloud and obscure. It is needless to show the sun shining, which will break out of itself. Yet when just occasion is offered he shows his perfections soundly though seldom, and then gracest them out to the best advantage.

In discourse he is neither too free, nor over-reserved, but observes a mediocrity. His hall is common to all comers, but his closet is locked. General matters he is as liberal to impart, as careful to conceal importances.

He trusteth not any with a secret which may endanger his estate.   For if he tells it to his servant, he makes him his master ; if to his friend, he enables him to be a foe, and to undo him at pleasure, whose secrecy he must buy at the party's own price, and if ever he shuts his purse, the other opens his mouth.

Matters of inferior consequence he will communicate to a fast friend, and crave his advice ; for two eyes see more than one, though it be never so big, and set, as in Polyphemus, in the midst of the forehead.

He is careful and provident in the managing of his private estate. Well may princes suspect those states-men not to be wise in the business of the common-wealth who are fools in ordering their own affairs. Our politician, if he enlargeth not his own estate, at least keeps it in good repair. As for avaricious courses he disdaineth them.   Sir Thomas More, though some years lord-chancellor of England, scarce left his son five-and-twenty pounds a year more than his father left him.   And Sir Henry Sidney (father to Sir Philip,) being lord-president of Wales and Ireland, got not one foot of land in either country, rather seeking after the common good than his private profit. I must confess the last age produced an English statesman who was the picklock of the cabinets of foreign princes, who, though the wisest

K

in his time and way, died poor and indebted to private men, though not so much as the whole kingdom was indebted to him.   But such an accident is rare ; and a small hospital will hold those statesmen who have impaired their means, not by their private carelessness, but carefulness for the public.

As for his carriage towards home-persons, he studieth men's natures, first reading the title pages of them by the report of fame ; but credits not fame's relations to the full.   Wherefore, to be more accurate he reads the chapters of men's natures, chiefly his concurrents and competitors, by the reports of their friends and foes, making allowances for their engagements, not believing all in the mass, but only what he judiciously extracteth.   Yet virtues confessed by their foes, and vices acknowledged by their friends, are commonly true.

In court factions he keeps himself in a free neutrality.   Otherwise to engage himself needlessly, were both folly and danger.   Yet he counts neutrality profaneness in such matters wherein God, his prince, the church, or state, are concerned.   Indeed, *he that meddleth with strife not belonging unto him, is like one that taketh a dog by the ears.*[1]   Yet if the dog

[1] Prov. xxvi. 17.

worrieth a sheep, we may, yea ought to rescue it from
his teeth, and must be champions for innocence when
it is overborne with might.   He that will stand neuter
in such matters of moment, wherein his calling commands him to be a party, with Servilius in Rome,
will please neither side : neutrality in matters of an indifferent nature may fit well, but never suit well in
important matters of far different conditions.

He is the centre wherein lines of intelligence meet
from all foreign countries.   He is careful that his
outlandish instructions be full, true, and speedy ; not
with the sluggard telling for news at noon, that the
sun is risen.

His masterpiece is in negotiating for his own master
with foreign princes.   At Rhodes there was a conten-
tion betwixt Apelles and Protogenes, co-rivals in the
mystery of limning.   Apelles, with his pencil, drew a
very slender even line ; Protogenes drew another
more small and slender, in the midst thereof with
another colour : Apelles again, with a third line of a
different colour, drew through the midst of what
Protogenes had made : thus our statesman traverseth
matters, doubling and redoubling in his foreign nego-
tiations with the politicians of other princes.

To conclude, some plead that dissembling is lawful
in state-craft, upon the presupposition that men must

meet with others who dissemble. Yea they hold, that thus to counterfeit, *se defendendo*, against a crafty co-rival, is no sin, but a just punishment on our adversary, who first began it. For my part, I confess that herein I rather see what, than whither to fly. But what shall I say? they need to have steady heads who can dive into these gulfs of policy, and come out with a safe conscience. I will look no longer on these whirlpools of state, lest my pen turn giddy.

THE GOOD JUDGE.

The good advocate, whom we formerly described, is since, by his prince's favour and own deserts, advanced to be a judge.

He is patient and attentive in hearing the pleadings on both sides ; and hearkens to the witnesses, though tedious. He may give a waking testimony who hath but a dreaming utterance, and many country people must be impertinent before they can be pertinent, and cannot give evidence about a hen, but first they must begin with it in the egg. All of which our judge is contented to hearken to.

He meets not a testimony half-way, but stays till it come at him. He that proceeds on half evidence will not do quarter justice.   Our judge will not go till he is led.

Having heard with patience, he gives sentence with uprightness.   For when he puts on his robes, he put off his relations to any, and, like Melchisedec, becomes without pedigree   His private affections are swallowed up in the common cause, as rivers lose their names in the ocean.   He therefore allows no noted favourites, which cannot but cause multification of fees, and suspicion of by-ways.

He silences that lawyer who seeks to set the neck of a bad cause, once broken with a definite sentence.

He so hates bribes that he is jealous to receive any kindness above the ordinary proportion of friendship ; lest like the sermons of wandering preachers, they should end in begging, and surely integrity is the proper portion of a judge.   Men have a touchstone whereby to try gold, but gold is the touchstone whereby to try men.

When he sits upon life, in judgment he remembereth mercy.   Then, they say, a butcher may not be of the jury, much less let him be the judge.   Oh let him take heed how he strikes that hath a dead hand.

If the cause be difficult, his diligence is the greater to sift it out.   For though there be mention (Psal. xxxvii. 6) of righteousness as clear as the noonday, yet God forbid that innocency which is no clearer than twilight, should be condemned. And seeing one's oath commands another's life, he searcheth whether malice did not command that oath: yet when all is done, the judge may be deceived by false evidence. But blame not the hand of the dial if it points at a false hour, when the fault is in the wheels of the clock which direct it and are out of frame.

The sentence of condemnation he pronounceth with all gravity. It is best when steeped in the judge's tears. He avoideth all jesting on men in misery: easily may he put them out of countenance whom he hath power to put out of life.

Such as are unworthy to live, and yet unfitted to die, he provides shall be instructed. By God's mercy, and good teaching, the reprieve of their bodies may get the pardon of their souls, and one day's longer life for them here may procure a blessed eternity for them hereafter.

He is exact to do justice in civil suits betwixt sovereign and subject. He counts the rules of state and laws of the realm mutually support each other. Those who made the laws to be not only desperate, but even opposite terms to maxims of government, were true friends neither to laws nor government. Extremity makes the next the best remedy. Extraordinary courses are not ordinarily to be used, when not enforced by absolute necessity.

And thus we leave our judge to receive a just reward of his integrity from the Judge of judges, at the great assize of the world.

THE GOOD BISHOP.

He is an overseer of a flock of shepherds, as a minister is of a flock of God's sheep. Divine providence and his prince's bounty advanced him to the place, whereof he was no whit ambitious: only he counts it good manners to sit there where God has placed him, though it be higher than he conceives himself to deserve, and hopes that he who called him to the office hath, or will in some measure fit him for it.

His life is so spotless, that malice is angry with him, because she cannot be angry with him : because she can find no just cause to accuse him. Our bishop takes no notice of the false accusations of people · disaffected against his order, but walks on circumspectly in his calling.

With his honour, his holiness and humility doth increase. His great place makes not his piety the less ; far be it from him that the glittering of the candlestick should dim the shining of his candle. The meanest minister of God's word may have free access unto him : whosoever brings a good cause brings his own welcome with him. The pious poor may enter in at his wide gates, when not so much as his wicket shall be open to wealthy unworthiness.

He is diligent and faithful in preaching the gospel : either by his pen, or by his vocal sermons, if age and other indispensable occasions hinder him not, teaching the clergy to preach, and the laity to live, according to the ancient canons. Object not that it is unfitting he should lie perdue, who is to walk the round, and that governing, as a higher employment, is to silence the preaching : for preaching is a principal part of governing, and Christ himself ruleth his church by his word. Hereby bishops should govern hearts, and make men yield unto them a true and willing obedience, reverencing God in them.

Painful, pious and peaceable ministers are his principal favourites. If he meets them in his way (yea he will make it his way to meet them) he bestoweth all grace and lustre upon them.

He is careful that church censures be justly and solemnly inflicted. He is careful and happy in suppressing of heresies and schisms. He distinguisheth of schismatics, as physicians do of leprous people : some are infectious, others not. He is very merciful in punishing offenders. He had rather draw tears than blood. And though the highest detestation of sin best agreeth with clergymen, yet ought they to cast a severe eye on the vice and example, and a merciful eye on the person.

He is very careful on whom he layeth hands in ordination ; lest afterwards he hath just cause to beshrew his fingers. For the sufficiency of scholarship he goeth by his own eye ; but for their honest life, he is guided by other men's hands, which would not so often deceive him, were testimonials a matter of less courtesy and more conscience. For whosoever subscribes them enters into bond to God and the church under heavy forfeiture, to avouch the honesty of the parties commended.

He meddleth as little as may be with temporal matters : having little skill in them, and less will to them, not that he is unworthy to manage them, but they unworthy to be managed by him. Yea, generally the most dexterous in spiritual matters are left-handed in temporal business, and go but untowardly about them. Wherefore our bishop *meddleth little in civil affairs, being out of his profession and element.* Heaven is his vocation, and therefore he counts earthly

employments avocations ; except in such cases which
lie, as I may say, in the marches of divinity, and have
connexion with his calling ; or else when temporal
matters meddle with him, so that he must rid them
out of his way. Yea he rather admireth than con-
demneth such of his brethren who are strengthened
with that which would distract him, making the con-
currence of spiritual and temporal power in them
support one another, and using worldly business as
their recreation to heavenly employment.

He is loved and feared of all, and his presence
frights the swearer either out of his oaths or into
silence, and he stains all other men's lives with the
clearness of his own.

Yet he daily prayeth God to keep him in so slip-
pery a place. Elisha prayed that a double portion
of Elijah's spirit might rest upon him. A father
descanteth hereon, that a double portion of grace was
necessary for Elisha, who was gracious at court, lived
in a plentiful way, and favoured of the kings of
Israel: whereas Elijah lived poorly and privately:
and more wisdom is requisite to manage prosperity
than affliction.

He is hospitable in his housekeeping according to
his estate. His bounty is with discretion to those
that deserve it : charity mistakes which relieves idle

people. The rankness of his housekeeping produces no riot in his family. St. Paul calls a Christian family well ordered, *a church in their house*. If a private man's house be a parochial, a bishop's may seem a cathedral church, as much better as bigger, so decently all things therein are disposed.

THE TRUE NOBLEMAN.

He is a gentleman in a text letter, because bred and living in a higher and larger way. Conceive him, when young, brought up at school, where he seriously applied himself to learning, and afterwards coming to his estate thus behaves himself.

Goodness sanctifies his greatness, and greatness supports his goodness. He improves the upper ground whereon he stands, thereby to do God the more glory.

He counts not care for his country's good to be beneath his state. Because he is a great pillar, shall he therefore bear the less weight, never meddling with matters of justice? Can this be counted too low for a lord, which is high enough for a king? Our nobleman freely serves his country, counting his very work a sufficient reward. (As by our laws no duke, earl, baron, or baronet, though justices of the peace, may take any wages at sessions.[1]) Yea, he detesteth all gainful ways, which have the least blush of dishonour.

He is careful in the thrifty managing of his estate. Gold though the most solid and heavy of metals, yet may be beaten out so thin as to be the lightest and slightest of all things. Thus nobility, though in itself most honourable, may be so attenuated through the smallness of means, as thereby to grow neglected, which makes our nobleman to practise Solomon's precept. *Be diligent to know the state of thy flocks, and look well to thine herds ; for the crown doth not endure to every generation.*[2] If not the crown, much less the coronet ; and good husbandry may as well stand with great honour as breadth may consist with height.

If a weak estate be left him by his ancestors, he seeks to repair it, by thrifty ways, yet noble : as by travelling, sparing abroad, till his state at home may outgrow debts and pensions : hereby he gains experience, and saves expense. Sometimes being private, sometimes shewing himself at a half light, and sometimes appearing like himself as occasion requires.

In proportion to his means he keeps a liberal house.

---

[1] Statute 14 of Ric. II. c. 11.   [2] Prov. xxvii. 23.

Our nobleman is especially careful to see all things discharged which he taketh up. When the corpse of Thomas Howard, second duke of Norfolk, was carried to be interred in the abbey of Thetford, anno 1524, no person could demand of him one groat for debt, or restitution for any injury done by him.[1]

His servants are best known by the coat and cognizance of their civil behaviour. He hateth all oppression of his tenants and neighbours. All the country are his retainers in love and observance. When they come to wait on him, they leave not their hearts at home behind them, but come willingly to tender their respects.

Some privileges of noblemen he endeavours to deserve, namely such privileges as are completely noble, that so his merits as well as the law should allow them unto him. He conceives this word, *on mine honour*, wraps up a great deal in it; which unfolded and then measured, will be found to be a large attestation, and no less than an elliptical oath, calling God to witness, who hath bestowed that honour upon him.

[1] Weaver's " Fun. Mon.," p. 839.

THE COURT LADY.

To describe a holy state without a virtuous lady therein, were to paint out a year without a spring : we come therefore to her character.

She sets not her face so often by her glass, as she composeth her soul by God's word. Which hath all the excellent qualities of a glass indeed. This glass hath power to smooth the wrinkles, cleanse the spots, and mend the faults it discovers.

She walks humbly before God in all religious duties. She is most constant and diligent at her hours of private prayer.

She is careful and most tender of her credit and reputation. There is a tree in Mexicana, which is so exceedingly tender that a man cannot touch any of its branches, but it withers presently.[1] A lady's credit is of equal niceness, a small touch may wound and kill it ; which makes her very cautious what company she keeps.

Yet she is not more careful of her own credit than of God's glory ; and stands up valiantly in the

---

[1] Doctor Heylen's "Microcos," p. 783.

defence thereof. If our lady hears any speaking disgracefully of God or of religion, she counts herself bound by her tenure (whereby she holds possession of grace here, and reversion of glory hereafter) to assert and vindicate the honour of the King of heaven, whose champion she professeth to be. One may be a lamb in private wrongs but in bearing general affronts to goodness, they are asses who are not lions.

She is pitiful and bountiful to people in distress.

She is a good scholar, and well learned in useful authors. Indeed, as in purchases, a house is valued at nothing, because it returneth no profit, and requires great charges to maintain it ; so for the same reasons, learning in a woman is little to be prized. But as for great ladies, who ought to be a confluence of rarities and perfections, some learning in them is not only useful, but necessary.

In discourse, her words are rather fit than fine, very choice and yet not chosen. Though her language be not gaudy, yet the plainness thereof pleaseth ; it is so proper and handsomely put on.

She affects not the vanity of foolish fashions ; but is decently apparelled according to her state and condition.

She is contented with that beauty which God hath

given her. If very handsome, no whit the more proud, but far the more thankful ; if unhandsome, she labours to better it in the virtues of her mind, that what is but plain cloth without, may be rich plush within. Indeed such natural defects as hinder her comfortable serving of God in her calling, may be amended by art ; and any member of the body being defective, may thereby be lawfully supplied. Thus glass eyes may be used, though not for seeing, for sightliness. But our lady detesteth all adulterate complexions, finding no precedent thereof in the Bible, save one, and her so bad, that ladies would blush through their paint, to make her the pattern of their imitation.

In her marriage she principally respects virtue and religion ; and next that, other accommodations, as we have formerly discoursed of. And she is careful in match not to bestow herself unworthily beneath her own degree to an ignoble person, except in case of necessity. Thus the gentlewomen in Champaigne, in France, some three hundred years since, were enforced to marry yeomen and farmers, because all the nobility in the country were slain in the wars, in the two voyages of King Lewis to Palestine : and thereupon ever since, by custom and privilege, the gentlewomen of Champaigne and Brye ennoble their husbands, and give them honour in marrying them, how mean soever before.[1]

Though pleasantly affected she is not transported with court delights. In her reduced thoughts she makes all the sport she hath seen, earnest to herself. It must be a dry flower indeed out of which the bee sucks no honey. They are the best Origens who do allegorize all earthly vanities into heavenly truths.

THE GOOD GENERAL.

The soldier, whom we formerly described, hath since, by the stairs of his own deserts, climbed up to be a general, and now we come to character him.

He is pious in the ordering of his own life. Some falsely conceive that religion spoileth the spirit of a general, as bad as a rainy day doth his plume of feathers, making it droop and hang down; whereas, indeed piety, only begets true prowess.

He acknowledgeth God the generalissimo of all armies; who in all battles, though the numbers be never so unequal, reserves the casting vote for himself.

He hath gained skill in his place by long experience;

---

[1] Andr. Favin. in his "Theatre of Honour," book i. chap. 6.

L

not beginning to lead others before himself ever knew
to follow, having never before, except in cock-matches,
beheld any battles. Surely they leap best in their
providence forward who fetch their rise farthest backward in their experience.

He either is, or is presumed, valiant. Indeed,
courage in him is necessary, though some think that
a general is above valour, who may command others
to be so ; as if it were all one whether courage were
his naturally, or by adoption, who can make the
valiant deeds of others seem his own; and his reputation for personal manhood once raised, will bear itself
up ; like a round body, some force is required to set
it, but a touch will keep it agoing; indeed it is extreme
indiscretion, except in extremities, for him to be
prodigal of his person.

He loves and is beloved of his soldiers, whose good
will he attaineth.

1. By giving them good words in his speeches unto
them. When wages have sometimes accidentally fallen
short, soldiers have accepted the payment in the fair
language and promise of their general.

2. By partaking with his soldiers in their painful
employments. When the English, at the Spanish
fleet's approach in eighty-eight, drew their ships out
of Plymouth haven, the Lord Admiral Howard him-

self towed a cable, the least joint of whose exemplary hand drew more than twenty men besides.

3. By sharing with them in their wants. When victuals have grown scant, some generals have pinched themselves to the same fare with their soldiers, who could not complain that their mess was bad, whilst their general was fellow commoner with them.

4. By taking notice, and rewarding of their deserts; never disinheriting a worthy soldier of his birthright, of the next office due unto him; for a worthy man is wounded more deeply by his own general's neglect than by his enemies' sword : the latter may kill him, but the former deadens his courage, or, which is worse, maddens it into discontent; who had rather others should make a ladder of his dead corpse to scale a city by it, than a bridge of him whilst alive for his punies to give him the go-by, and pass over him to preferment.

He is fortunate in what he undertakes. Such a one was Julius Cæsar, who in Britain, a country undiscovered, peopled by a valiant nation, began a war in autumn without apparent advantage, not having any intelligence there, being to pass over the sea into a colder climate (an enterprise, saith one, well worthy the invincible courage of Cæsar, but not of his accustomed prudence), and yet returned victorious. Indeed

God is the sole disposer of success ; other gifts he also scattereth amongst men, yet so that they themselves scramble to gather them up, whereas success God gives immediately into their hands on who he pleaseth to bestow it.

He trieth the forces of a new enemy before he encounters him. Samson is half conquered when it is known where his strength lies ; and skirmishes are scouts for the discovery of the strength of an army before battle be given.

He makes his flying enemy a bridge of gold, and disarms them of their best weapon, which is necessity to fight whether they will or no. Men forced to a battle against their intention, often conquer beyond their expectation : stop a flying coward, and he will turn his legs into arms, and lay about him manfully : whereas, open him a passage to escape, and he will quickly shut up his courage.

But surely a corslet is no canonical coat for me, nor suits it with my clergy profession to proceed any further in this warlike description.

The King.

He is a mortal god. We will describe him, first as ✓
a good man, so was Henry the Third ; then as a good
king, so was Richard the Third, both which meeting
together make a king complete. For he that is not *a
good man*, or *but a good man*, can never be a good
sovereign.

He is temperate in the ordering of his own life. O
the mandate of a king's example is able to do much.
He holds his crown immediately from the God of
heaven. Yea, the character of loyalty to kings so
deeply impressed in subjects' hearts, shows that only
God's finger wrote it there. Hence it is if one chance
to conceive ill of his sovereign, though within the
cabinet of his soul, presently his own heart grows
jealous of his own heart, and he could wish the tongue
cut out of his tell-tale thoughts lest they should accuse
themselves. And though sometimes rebels (atheists
against the God on earth) may labour to obliterate
loyalty in them, yet even then their conscience, the
king's attorney, frames articles against them, and they
stand in daily fear lest Darius Longimanus (such a one
is every king) should reach them, and revenge himself.

He improves his power to defend true religion. He useth mercy and justice in his proceedings against offenders.   Solomon saith, *the throne is established by justice:* and Solomon saith, *the throne is upholden by mercy.*   Which two proverbs speak no more contradiction, than he that saith that the two opposite side walls of a house hold up the same roof.   In his mercy, our king desires to resemble the God of heaven, who measureth his judgments by the ordinary cubit ; but his kindnesses by the cubit of the sanctuary, twice as big : yea all the world had been a hell without God's mercy.

He is rich in having a plentiful exchequer of his people's hearts : for love, the key of hearts, will open the closest coffers.   Meantime how poor is that prince, amidst all his wealth, whose subjects are only kept by a slavish fear the jailer of the soul.

He willingly orders his actions by the laws of his realm, our king loves to be legal in all his practices. He also hearkeneth to the advice of good counsellors, yet withal is careful to maintain his just prerogative, that as it be not outstretched, so it may not be over-shortened.

FINIS.